Mastermaths 1

Paul Briten

Head of St. Stephen's School, Twickenham

Oxford University Press

Oxford University Press, Walton Street, Oxford OX2 6DP

Oxford is a trade mark of Oxford University Press

©Paul Briten 1984 ISBN 0 19 834743 X

First published 1984
Reprinted 1985, 1988, 1989, 1990, 1992

Typeset by Tradespools Ltd, Frome; illustrated by CGS Studios, Cheltenham
Printed in Hong Kong

Contents

Contents

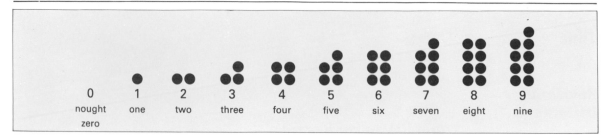

0	1	2	3	4	5	6	7	8	9
nought zero	one	two	three	four	five	six	seven	eight	nine

A How many men in each boat?

B How many boats?

C How many dots?

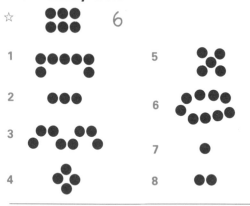

D Draw a line of:

☆ 9 dots ●●●●●●●●●

1 4 dots   5 3 dots

2 2 dots   6 8 dots

3 7 dots   7 1 dot

4 5 dots   8 6 dots

E How many:

☆ pink fish?   4

1 white fish?   3 black fish?

2 red fish?

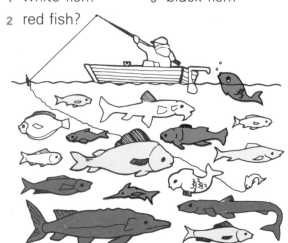

	0	1	2	3	4	5	6	7	8	9
	nought zero	one	two	three	four	five	six	seven	eight	nine

counting on ——→   ←—— **counting back**

A Copy and complete:

☆ 0 ✳ ✳ 3 ✳ ✳ 6
  0 1 2 3 4 5 6

1 0 ✳ 2 ✳ 4 ✳ 6
2 3 ✳ 5 ✳ ✳ 8 9
3 2 ✳ ✳ 5 ✳ ✳ 8
4 4 ✳ ✳ ✳ 8 ✳
5 ✳ ✳ 2 ✳ ✳ ✳ 6
6 1 ✳ ✳ ✳ ✳ ✳ 7

D Copy and complete:

☆ 8 ✳ ✳ ✳ 4 ✳ ✳
  8 7 6 5 4 3 2

1 9 ✳ 7 ✳ ✳ ✳ 3
2 7 ✳ ✳ 4 ✳ ✳ 1
3 9 ✳ ✳ 6 ✳ ✳ ✳
4 8 ✳ ✳ 5 ✳ ✳ ✳
5 ✳ ✳ 4 ✳ ✳ 1 ✳
6 ✳ 5 ✳ ✳ ✳ ✳ 0

B Write these numbers in order, **smallest first**:

☆ 3 7 1 8 9
  1 3 7 8 9

1 6 1 3 5 4
2 7 2 8 3 9
3 6 3 0 5 4
4 1 3 7 0 5
5 9 5 3 8 1 2
6 4 8 6 1 7 0

E Write these numbers in order, **largest first**:

☆ 4 7 3 9 1
  9 7 4 3 1

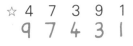

1 7 5 9 6 8
2 2 7 9 4 5
3 3 2 6 4 8
4 6 3 5 0 7
5 1 4 0 9 6 3
6 8 3 0 5 9 1

C Write the number that is **one more than**:

☆ three 4

1 six   4 two   7 five
2 four   5 one   8 zero
3 eight   6 seven

F Write the number that is **one less than**:

☆ seven 6

1 nine   4 two   7 one
2 three   5 eight   8 six
3 four   6 five

How many counters altogether?

Write: **5 + 3 = 8**
Say: 'five add three equals eight'

How many counters altogether?

four add three equals seven
4 + 3 = 7

A How many counters altogether:

☆  4+3=7

1

2

3

4

5

6

7

8

9

10

B Use counters if you need to.
Write numbers for ✳'s:

☆ 4+1=✳ 5

1 3+1=✳   8 1+7=✳
2 2+2=✳   9 3+3=✳
3 1+6=✳   10 4+4=✳
4 6+3=✳   11 3+2=✳
5 3+4=✳   12 2+3=✳
6 5+4=✳   13 5+2=✳
7 8+1=✳   14 2+5=✳

C Write in **figures** and **signs**:

☆ three add two equals five
   3+2=5

1 two add four equals six
2 five add one equals six
3 four add two equals six
4 seven add one equals eight
5 two add six equals eight
6 eight add nought equals eight
7 three add six equals nine
8 six add three equals nine

D Write numbers for ✳'s:

☆ six add two equals ✳ 8
1 five add three equals ✳
2 one add seven equals ✳
3 three add three equals ✳
4 four add nought equals ✳
5 two add six equals ✳
6 five add four equals ✳
7 four add five equals ✳
8 four add four equals ✳

E Write numbers for ✳'s:

☆ 6+3=✳ 9
1 4+3=✳   6 1+1=✳
2 2+4=✳   7 6+0=✳
3 1+4=✳   8 5+4=✳
4 0+4=✳   9 0+3=✳
5 2+2=✳   10 1+8=✳

5+3=8
3+5=8

The sign $<$ means **is less than**
The sign $>$ means **is greater than**

4 $<$ 9 means '4 is less than 9'

6+2 $>$ 5 means '6+2 is greater than 5'
       or   **8 is greater than 5**

A Use counters if you need to.
Write numbers for ✲'s:

☆ 4+2=✲   6
   2+4=✲   6

1 6+1=✲   **6** 4+3=✲
   1+6=✲   3+4=✲

2 5+4=✲   **7** 2+6=✲
   4+5=✲   6+2=✲

3 7+2=✲   **8** 3+0=✲
   2+7=✲   0+3=✲

4 4+0=✲   **9** 5+2=✲
   0+4=✲   2+5=✲

5 3+2=✲   **10** 8+1=✲
   2+3=✲   1+8=✲

B Write numbers for ✲'s:

☆ 6+✲=9   3

1 4+3=✲   **9** 9+0=✲
2 3+✲=7   **10** 0+✲=9
3 2+6=✲   **11** 1+7=✲
4 6+✲=8   **12** ✲+1=8
5 7+✲=9   **13** 6+3=✲
6 ✲+7=9   **14** 3+✲=9
7 3+2=✲   **15** 3+✲=8
8 2+✲=5   **16** 5+✲=8

C Write the sign $<$ or $>$ for ✲'s:

☆ 7✲5 $>$

1 3✲6   **9** 6✲9
2 9✲4   **10** 6✲4
3 8✲3   **11** 5✲6
4 0✲1   **12** 1✲8
5 7✲5   **13** 6✲5
6 4✲2   **14** 1✲7
7 7✲8   **15** 0✲9
8 2✲4   **16** 8✲2

D Write the sign $<$ or $>$ for ✲'s:

☆ 6✲5+2 $<$

1 3+1✲6   **11** 5✲4+2
2 2+5✲9   **12** 6✲5+4
3 4+4✲7   **13** 9✲6+2
4 3+5✲7   **14** 2✲4+2
5 8+1✲2   **15** 0✲4+0
6 0+5✲7   **16** 7✲6+3
7 4+5✲3   **17** 3✲4+3
8 6+2✲9   **18** 1✲3+3
9 2+2✲1   **19** 4✲2+3
10 1+6✲8   **20** 8✲5+4

> is greater than

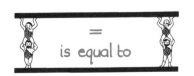

= is equal to

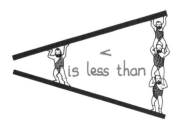

< is less than

5 blocks . . .

. . . take away 2   . . . 3 left

You can use subtraction to take away.
Write: **5−2=3**

Take away **4** counters from this group:

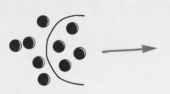

How many are left? **5**
Write: **9−4=5**

A Write how many are left:

☆ 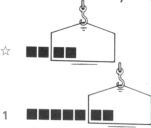 $4-2=2$

1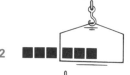

2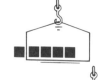

3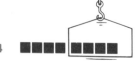

4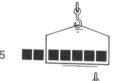

5

6

7

8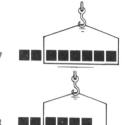

B How many counters are left if you:

☆ take away 3?

 $7-3=4$

1 take away 2?   6 take away 2?

2 take away 4?   7 take away 4?

3 take away 5?   8 take away 6?

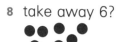

4 take away 3?   9 take away 8?

5 take away 6?   10 take away 5?

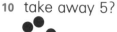

C Use counters if you need to.
Write numbers for ✳'s:

☆ 8−2= ✳ 6

1 7−4= ✳   6 9−6= ✳

2 8−1= ✳   7 7−5= ✳

3 6−4= ✳   8 8−7= ✳

4 9−5= ✳   9 7−5= ✳

5 8−7= ✳   10 9−9= ✳

 penny 1p

 two pence 2p

 five pence 5p

A Name these coins:

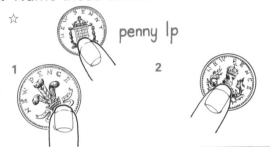

☆ penny 1p

1

2

B How much money in each bag?

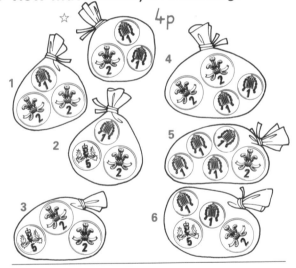

☆ 4p

1

2

3

4

5

6

C How much altogether?

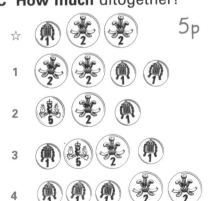

☆ 5p

1

2

3

4

D How much money?

☆ 2p+5p=✳ 7p

1 2p+2p=✳   6 4p+3p=✳
2 1p+5p=✳   7 2p+6p=✳
3 5p+2p=✳   8 5p+4p=✳
4 5p+2p+1p=✳   9 7p+1p=✳
5 2p+1p+2p=✳   10 5p+3p+1p=✳

E 2p is taken from each box.
How much is left?

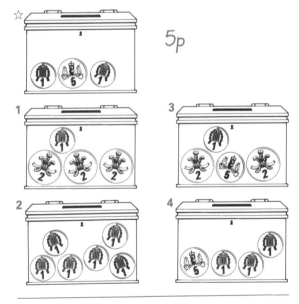

☆ 5p

1

3

2

4

F How much is left when:

☆ Mike has 9p and spends 4p? 5p
1 Mary has 8p and spends 3p?
2 Jo has 7p and spends 5p?
3 Paula has 6p and spends 2p?
4 Jim has 9p and spends 8p?
5 Ann has 7p and spends 7p?

complementary addition

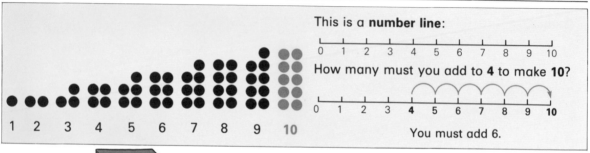

This is a **number line**:

How many must you add to **4** to make **10**?

You must add 6.

A 1 box holds 10 pencils.

How many more pencils to fill each box?

☆ 2

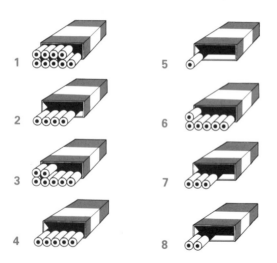

C How many must you add to these numbers to make 10?

☆ eight   2

1 nine   4 one   7 three

2 seven   5 six   8 nought

3 five   6 two

D Use coins if you need to.
There should be 10p in each box.
How much is missing?

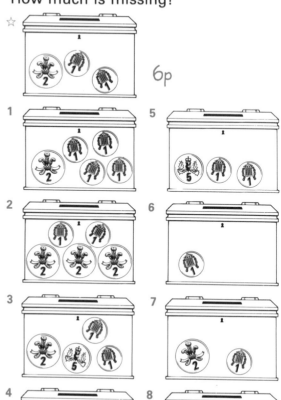

☆ 6p

B Copy and complete:

☆ 3	*	*	6	*	*	9	10
3	4	5	6	7	8	9	10

1	0	*	*	3	*	5	*
2	4	*	*	7	*	*	10
3	2	*	4	*	*	7	*
4	5	*	*	8	*	*	
5	*	1	*	*	4	*	*
6	4	*	*	*	*	9	*

Numbers to 10

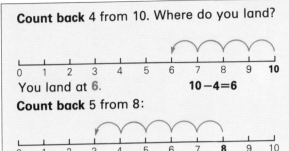

Count back 4 from 10. Where do you land?

You land at **6**.   **10−4=6**

Count back 5 from 8:

8−5=3

ten, nine, eight
seven, six, five,
four, three,
two, one,
zero . . .

A Where do you land when you **count back**:

☆ 5 from 9?

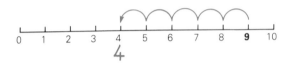

4

1 4 from 7?

2 3 from 8?

3 2 from 9?

4 3 from 7?

5 5 from 10?

6 4 from 9?

7 6 from 10?

8 4 from 10?

B Pencils come in boxes of ten.

How many left when:

☆ 3 are taken? 7

1 2 are taken?   **6** 0 are taken?

2 6 are taken?   **7** 8 are taken?

3 5 are taken?   **8** 10 are taken?

4 1 is taken?   **9** 7 are taken?

5 4 are taken?   **10** 9 are taken?

C Write numbers for ✱'s:

☆ 7−2=✱   5

1 6−3=✱   **6** 9−3=✱

2 5−1=✱   **7** 10−6=✱

3 7−4=✱   **8** 9−7=✱

4 8−3=✱   **9** 10−4=✱

5 8−5=✱   **10** 5−4=✱

D How many marbles are left if:

☆ Jo has 8 and loses 5? 3

1 Mary has 7 and loses 3?

2 Jim has 5 and loses 4?

3 Ann has 10 and loses 3?

4 Jill has 9 and loses 6?

5 Mike has 10 and loses 5?

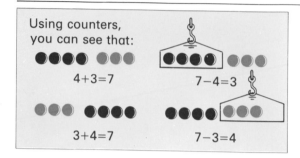

Using counters, you can see that:

$4+3=7$

$7-4=3$

$3+4=7$

$7-3=4$

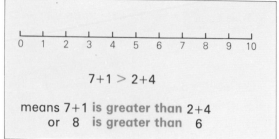

$7+1 > 2+4$

means 7+1 is greater than 2+4
or   8   is greater than   6

A Use counters if you need to.
Write numbers for ✱'s:

☆ ●●●●● ●●●
$5+3=$ ✱   8
$3+5=$ ✱   8
$8-3=$ ✱   5
$8-$ ✱ $=3$ 5

1 ●●●● ●●
$4+2=$ ✱
$2+$ ✱ $=6$
$6-4=$ ✱
$6-$ ✱ $=4$

5 ●●●●●●● ●●
$7+$ ✱ $=9$
✱ $+7=9$
$9-2=$ ✱
$9-$ ✱ $=2$

2 ●●●●● ●●
$5+$ ✱ $=7$
✱ $+5=7$
$7-5=$ ✱
$7-2=$ ✱

6 ●● ●●●●●●●
$2+8=$ ✱
$8+$ ✱ $=10$
$10-$ ✱ $=2$
$10-$ ✱ $=8$

3 ●●●●●● ●●●
$6+$ ✱ $=9$
✱ $+6=9$
$9-$ ✱ $=3$
$9-$ ✱ $=6$

7 ●●● ●●●●
$3+4=$ ✱
$4+$ ✱ $=7$
$7-3=$ ✱
✱ $-4=3$

4 ●●● ●●
$3+$ ✱ $=5$
✱ $+3=5$
$5-$ ✱ $=2$
$5-2=$ ✱

8 ●●●● ●●●●●
$4+$ ✱ $=9$
$5+$ ✱ $=9$
$9-$ ✱ $=5$
✱ $-5=4$

B Write the sign > < or = for ✱'s:

☆ $6+3$ ✱ $2+5$ >
1 $2+6$ ✱ $4+1$
2 $9+0$ ✱ $3+2$
3 $4+3$ ✱ $3+4$
4 $7+1$ ✱ $2+4$
5 $2+7$ ✱ $8+2$
6 $4+4$ ✱ $3+5$
7 $7+2$ ✱ $2+7$
8 $6+4$ ✱ $3+6$
9 $5+3$ ✱ $3+5$
10 $4+1$ ✱ $1+5$
11 $6+2$ ✱ $7-3$
12 $8+1$ ✱ $8-1$
13 $6+3$ ✱ $3+6$
14 $8-5$ ✱ $8-3$
15 $4-2$ ✱ $4+2$
16 $6+4$ ✱ $4+6$

C How many birds must be added to each flock to make 10 altogether?

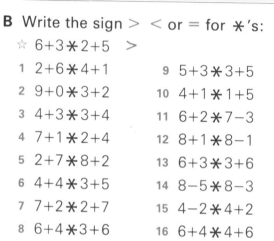

☆   3

1

2

3

D Write numbers for ✱'s:

☆ $8+$ ✱ $=10$ 2
1 $6+$ ✱ $=10$
2 $4+6=$ ✱
3 $7+$ ✱ $=10$
4 $3+7=$ ✱
5 $9+$ ✱ $=10$
6 $1+9=$ ✱
7 $4+$ ✱ $=10$
8 $2+$ ✱ $=10$
9 $0+$ ✱ $=10$
10 $1+$ ✱ $=10$
11 $5+$ ✱ $=10$
12 $3+$ ✱ $=10$

A Write these numbers in words:

1 6   6 7

2 8   7 1

3 10   8 3

4 5   9 9

5 2   10 0

B Write these numbers in order, **smallest first**:

1 6 9 1 10 5

2 4 7 1 9 2

3 10 6 0 5 4

4 3 2 8 9 1

5 0 9 5 3 10

6 5 2 7 10 6

7 3 8 0 5 1

8 10 6 3 7 0

C Write numbers for *'s:

1 4+3=*   8 2+6=*

2 3+4=*   9 5+5=*

3 5+2=*   10 9+0=*

4 2+6=*   11 1+8=*

5 6+3=*   12 0+10=*

6 7+2=*   13 3+5=*

7 4+5=*   14 6+4=*

D Write numbers for *'s:

1 9−3=*   8 9−6=*

2 7−5=*   9 5−2=*

3 8−6=*   10 8−5=*

4 10−3=*   11 9−5=*

5 6−5=*   12 7−2=*

6 8−0=*   13 8−3=*

7 7−7=*   14 6−0=*

E Write numbers for *'s:

1 6+*=8   6 3+*=10

2 2+*=4   7 3+*=7

3 1+*=8   8 6+*=10

4 4+*=10   9 8+*=8

5 5+*=8   10 1+*=10

F How much money in each bag?

1    3

2    4

G You have 10 pence.
How much left when you spend:

1 4 pence?   6 3 pence?

2 2 pence?   7 5 pence?

3 7 pence?   8 8 pence?

4 9 pence?   9 6 pence?

5 1 penny?   10 10 pence?

H Write the sign < or > for *'s:

1 8*6   6 7*2+3

2 3*10   7 4*3+5

3 3+2*7   8 2+1*3+2

4 4+1*8   9 4+5*6+2

5 6+3*8   10 6+1*8+2

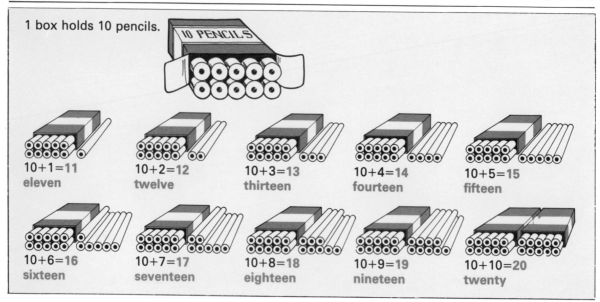

1 box holds 10 pencils.

10+1=11 eleven
10+2=12 twelve
10+3=13 thirteen
10+4=14 fourteen
10+5=15 fifteen

10+6=16 sixteen
10+7=17 seventeen
10+8=18 eighteen
10+9=19 nineteen
10+10=20 twenty

A Write in figures:

☆ thirteen 13

1 nineteen   6 twelve

2 eleven   7 twenty

3 fifteen   8 fourteen

4 eighteen   9 seventeen

5 sixteen   10 ten

B Write these numbers in words:

☆ 15 fifteen

1 13   5 14   8 17

2 19   6 18   9 11

3 12   7 10   10 20

4 16

C Write these numbers in tens and units:

☆ 11 1 ten 1 unit

1 12   6 19

2 13   7 17

3 14   8 18

4 15   9 10

5 16   10 20

D How many pencils in each group?

☆   16

1

2

3

4

E Write the number that is:

☆ 1 ten and 4 units   14

1 1 ten and 2 units   6 1 ten and 9 units

2 1 ten and 5 units   7 1 ten and 6 units

3 1 ten and 7 units   8 1 ten and 8 units

4 1 ten and 3 units   9 1 ten and 1 unit

5 1 ten and 0 units 10 2 tens and 0 units

0 1 2 3 4 5 6 7 8 9 10 11 12 13 14 15 16 17 18 19 20

A What number comes **between**:

☆ eleven and thirteen? 12

1 twelve and fourteen?

2 sixteen and eighteen?

3 ten and twelve?

4 seventeen and nineteen?

5 nine and eleven?

6 thirteen and fifteen?

7 nought and two?

8 eighteen and twenty?

B Write these numbers in order, **smallest first**:

☆ 12 14 7 9 11

7 9 11 12 14

1 13 8 5 11 10

2 16 17 20 19 15

3 8 12 10 9 11

4 16 14 11 9 15

5 6 15 0 20 12

6 18 2 14 9 20

C Write in words:

☆ 1 ten 6 units   sixteen

1 1 ten 4 units   6 1 ten 7 units

2 1 ten 1 unit   7 1 ten 2 units

3 1 ten 5 units   8 1 ten 8 units

4 1 ten 9 units   9 1 ten 0 units

5 1 ten 3 units   10 2 tens 0 units

D Write these numbers in tens and units:

☆ 18 1 ten and 8 units

1 15   6 20

2 17   7 16

3 11   8 12

4 19   9 10

5 14   10 13

E Use counters if you need to. Write numbers for ✳'s:

☆ $10+6=$✳ 16

1 $10+5=$✳   6 $10+8=$✳

2 $10+1=$✳   7 $10+2=$✳

3 $10+9=$✳   8 $10+7=$✳

4 $10+0=$✳   9 $10+4=$✳

5 $10+3=$✳   10 $10+10=$✳

F Write these numbers in order, **largest first**:

☆ 16 12 14 19 8

19 16 14 12 8

1 15 17 9 11 10

2 18 15 20 17 19

3 14 8 10 12 13

4 15 11 9 10 8

5 0 6 11 9 12

6 14 20 4 10 0

7 3 12 19 8 14

8 17 5 16 9 11

9 6 14 18 7 13

10 3 15 8 12 1

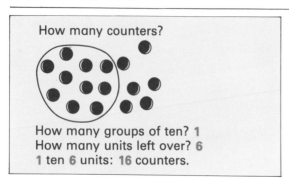

How many counters?

How many groups of ten? **1**
How many units left over? **6**
1 ten **6** units: **16** counters.

A Write how many counters in 2 different ways:

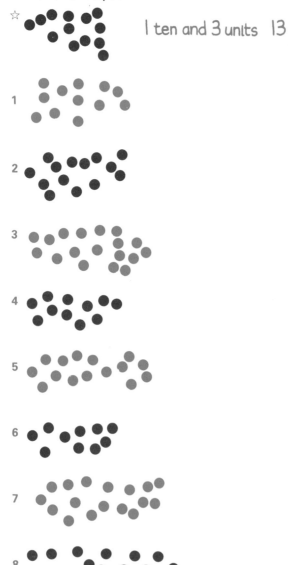

☆ I ten and 3 units 13

1

2

3

4

5

6

7

8

B Copy and complete this table:

☆	ten	10	I ten and 0 units	10+0
1	eleven			
2	twelve			
3	thirteen			
4	fourteen			
5	fifteen			
6	sixteen			
7	seventeen			
8	eighteen			
9	nineteen			
10	twenty			

C How many units altogether?

☆ 1 ten and 4 units 14 units

1 1 ten and 6 units 6 1 ten and 7 units
2 1 ten and 3 units 7 1 ten and 2 units
3 1 ten and 0 units 8 1 ten and 8 units
4 1 ten and 9 units 9 1 ten and 1 unit
5 1 ten and 5 units 10 2 tens and 0 units

D Sweets are put into packs of 10.
How many left over with:

☆ 12 sweets? 2

1 16 sweets? 6 10 sweets?
2 11 sweets? 7 13 sweets?
3 17 sweets? 8 20 sweets?
4 14 sweets? 9 15 sweets?
5 19 sweets? 10 18 sweets?

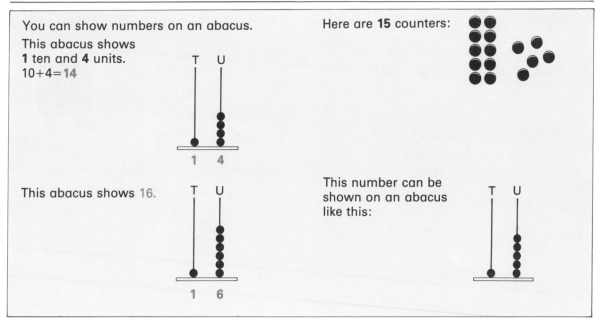

You can show numbers on an abacus.
This abacus shows
1 ten and **4** units.
10+4=**14**

Here are **15** counters:

This abacus shows 16.

This number can be shown on an abacus like this:

A Write the number shown on each abacus:

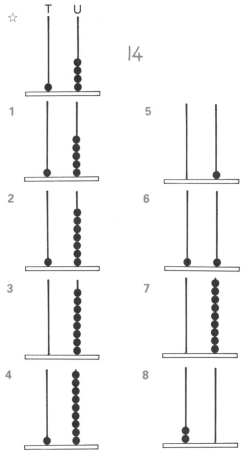

14

1

2

3

4

5

6

7

8

B Draw an abacus picture to show how many counters in each group:

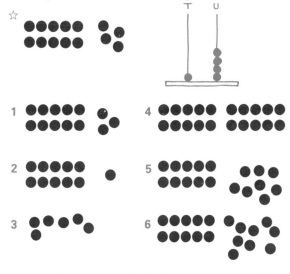

1

2

3

4

5

6

C Draw abacus pictures to show these numbers:

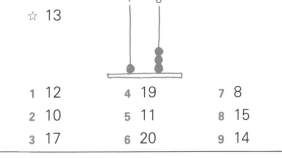

☆ 13

1 12   4 19   7 8
2 10   5 11   8 15
3 17   6 20   9 14

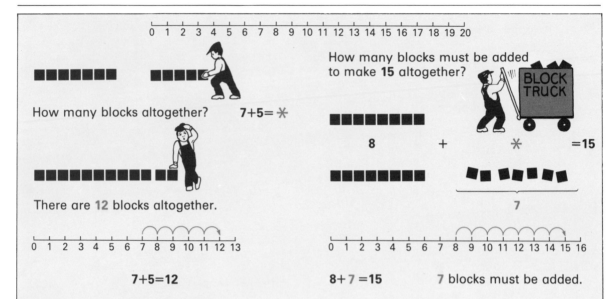

How many blocks altogether? 7+5= ✳

There are **12** blocks altogether.

7+5=12

How many blocks must be added to make **15** altogether?

8 + ✳ =15

7

8+ 7 =15   **7** blocks must be added.

A Write how many altogether:

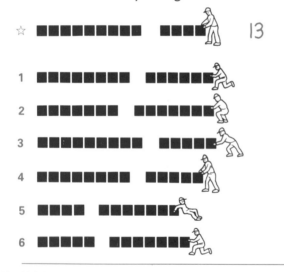

☆ 13

1

2

3

4

5

6

B Write numbers for ✳'s:

☆ 7+5= ✳   12

1 6+4= ✳	9 6+7= ✳
2 4+6= ✳	10 7+6= ✳
3 9+6= ✳	11 8+8= ✳
4 6+9= ✳	12 9+9= ✳
5 11+5= ✳	13 5+5= ✳
6 5+11= ✳	14 7+7= ✳
7 8+9= ✳	15 6+6= ✳
8 9+8= ✳	16 10+10= ✳

C How many blocks must be added to these piles to make 16 altogether?

☆  7

1

2

3

4

D Use a number line if you need to. Write numbers for ✳'s:

☆ 12+ ✳ =17   5

1 6+ ✳ =10	7 7+ ✳ =14
2 4+ ✳ =10	8 9+ ✳ =18
3 8+ ✳ =11	9 6+ ✳ =12
4 3+ ✳ =11	10 15+ ✳ =16
5 7+ ✳ =13	11 13+ ✳ =19
6 6+ ✳ =13	12 14+ ✳ =20

Numbers to 20

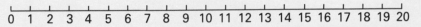

13 blocks......take away 7 ...leaves 6 blocks
$13-7=6$

There were **14** blocks. There are **5** left.
How many have been taken away?

$14- * =5$
$14- 9 =5$ There are **9** blocks in the box.

A Write how many are left:

☆
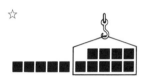

$14-9=5$

1

2
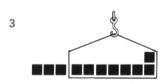

3

4

C There were 13 blocks.
How many have been taken away?

☆

10

1

2

3
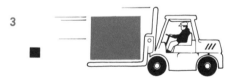

B Use a number line if you need to.
Write numbers for ✱'s:

☆ $12-6= *$ 6
1 $10-7= *$
2 $10-4= *$
3 $11-6= *$
4 $14-5= *$
5 $15-7= *$
6 $18-6= *$

7 $17-4= *$
8 $19-10= *$
9 $14-10= *$
10 $19-12= *$
11 $20-14= *$
12 $20-16= *$

D Use a number line if you need to.
Write numbers for ✱'s:

☆ $16- * =7$ 9
1 $12- * =8$
2 $12- * =4$
3 $15- * =6$
4 $15- * =9$
5 $17- * =6$
6 $17- * =11$

7 $19- * =10$
8 $20- * =14$
9 $16- * =8$
10 $13- * =6$
11 $14- * =8$
12 $20- * =11$

Using counters you can see that:

●●●●●●●●●○○○○○○ 9+6=15

●●●●●●○○○○○○○○○ 6+9=15

●●●●●●○○○○○○○○○ 15−9=6

●●●●●●○○○○○○○○○ 15−6=9

●●●●●●●●○○○○○○

If you know that 8+6=14,
you can write 3 more facts:
6+8=14   14−6=8   14−8=6

A Use counters if you need to.
Write numbers for ✳'s:

☆ ●●●●●●●● ●●●●●

8+5=✳ 13   13−8=✳ 5
5+8=✳ 13   13−✳=8 5

1 ●●●●●● ●●●●●●●

6+7=✳   13−6=✳
7+✳=13   13−✳=6

2 ●●●●● ●●●●●●

5+6=✳   11−✳=6
✳+5=11   11−✳=5

3 ●●●●●●● ●●●●●●●●

7+✳=15   15−✳=8
8+✳=15   15−✳=7

4 ●●●●●●●●● ●●●●●

9+5=✳   14−✳=5
5+✳=14   14−✳=9

5 ●●●●●●● ●●●●●●●●●

7+✳=16   16−✳=9
✳+7=16   16−9=✳

6 ●●●●●●●● ●●●●●●●●●

8+9=✳   17−✳=9
9+✳=17   17−9=✳

B Write 3 more facts for each of these:

☆ ●●●●●●● ●●●●●   5+7=12
7+5=12   12−7=5
                      12−5=7

1 ●●●●●●● ●●●●
7+4=11

2 ●●●●●●●● ●●●
8+3=11

3 ●●●●● ●●●●●●●
5+7=12

4 ●●●●●●●●● ●●●●
9+4=13

5 ●●●●●●● ●●●●●●●●
7+8=15

6 ●●●●●● ●●●●●●●●●
6+9=15

C How many socks must be added to
each line to make 18 altogether?

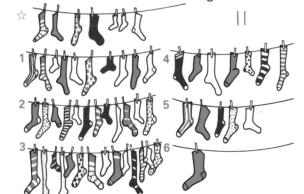

Numbers to 20

ten pence
10p

A How much money in each box?

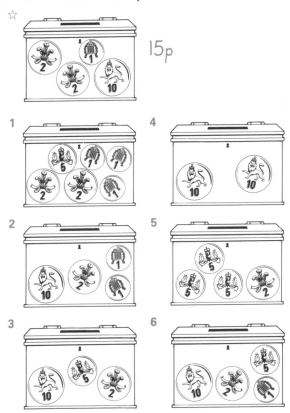

15p

B How much money?

☆ 4p+7p=✻ 11p

1 3p+6p=✻   7 8p+9p=✻
2 5p+5p=✻   8 10p+5p=✻
3 4p+8p=✻   9 11p+6p=✻
4 9p+5p=✻   10 9p+11p=✻
5 6p+8p=✻   11 12p+7p=✻
6 9p+7p=✻   12 10p+10p=✻

C What is the hidden coin in each bag?

2p

D Use coins if you need to.
How much left if:

☆ Ben has 12p and spends 5p?   7p
1 Paula has 10p and spends 3p?
2 Ann has 14p and spends 8p?
3 Jill has 18p and spends 10p?
4 Carl has 16p and spends 11p?
5 Kim has 19p and spends 14p?

E How much money?

☆ 15p−8p=✻   7p

1 10p−6p=✻   6 20p−7p=✻
2 10p−4p=✻   7 20p−12p=✻
3 12p−7p=✻   8 13p−9p=✻
4 13p−8p=✻   9 15p−7p=✻
5 14p−6p=✻   10 16p−8p=✻

A Write **in words** the number that is:

1 1 ten and 4 units   6 1 ten and 0 units

2 1 ten and 6 units   7 1 ten and 5 units

3 1 ten and 3 units   8 1 ten and 8 units

4 1 ten and 1 unit   9 2 tens and 0 units

5 1 ten and 7 units   10 1 ten and 9 units

B Write these numbers in order, smallest first:

1   16   7   12   10   4

2   19   14   2   17   10

3   11   12   15   1   8

4   16   6   5   14   20

5   13   2   15   4   17

C How many counters in these groups?

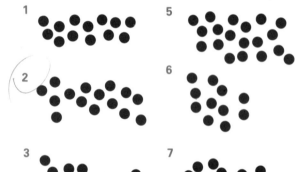
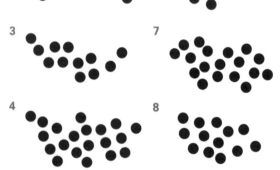

D Pencils are put into packs of 10. How many left over with:

1 16 pencils?   6 19 pencils?

2 12 pencils?   7 15 pencils?

3 11 pencils?   8 20 pencils?

4 18 pencils?   9 17 pencils?

5 10 pencils?   10 14 pencils?

E Write numbers for $*$'s:

1 $10+7=*$ 6 $14+5=*$

2 $13+5=*$ 7 $8+7=*$

3 $8+6=*$ 8 $9+9=*$

4 $7+9=*$ 9 $4+10=*$

5 $8+11=*$ 10 $16+3=*$

F Write numbers for $*$'s:

1 $16-7=*$ 6 $17-10=*$

2 $14-9=*$ 7 $18-8=*$

3 $20-10=*$ 8 $19-11=*$

4 $12-4=*$ 9 $15-7=*$

5 $13-8=*$ 10 $16-14=*$

G Write numbers for $*$'s:

1 $14+*=16$ 7 $15-*=12$

2 $9+*=15$ 8 $20-*=10$

3 $4+*=12$ 9 $18-*=9$

4 $11+*=18$ 10 $14-*=8$

5 $10+*=20$ 11 $16-*=9$

6 $8+*=8$ 12 $14-*=3$

H What is the hidden coin in each bag?

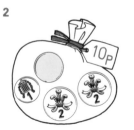

Numbers to 100

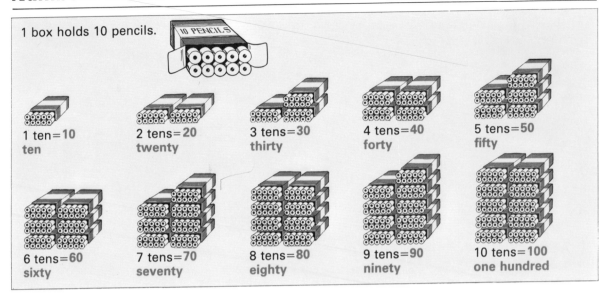

1 box holds 10 pencils.

1 ten = 10 — ten
2 tens = 20 — twenty
3 tens = 30 — thirty
4 tens = 40 — forty
5 tens = 50 — fifty
6 tens = 60 — sixty
7 tens = 70 — seventy
8 tens = 80 — eighty
9 tens = 90 — ninety
10 tens = 100 — one hundred

A Write in figures:

☆ fifty 50

1 thirty
2 seventy
3 one hundred
4 ten
5 forty
6 ninety
7 eighty
8 sixty
9 twenty

B Write these numbers as words:

☆ 60 sixty

1 90
2 10
3 40
4 30
5 20
6 100
7 70
8 80
9 50

C How many units in:

☆ 3 tens? thirty

1 5 tens?
2 9 tens?
3 1 ten?
4 8 tens?
5 7 tens?
6 2 tens?
7 4 tens?
8 6 tens?
9 10 tens?

D How many tens in:

☆ 40? 4

1 60?
2 30?
3 80?
4 10?
5 90?
6 50?
7 100?
8 70?
9 20?

E Write these numbers as words:

☆ 6 tens 0 units sixty

1 4 tens 0 units
2 7 tens 0 units
3 9 tens 0 units
4 3 tens 0 units
5 8 tens 0 units
6 5 tens 0 units
7 10 tens 0 units
8 2 tens 0 units
9 1 ten 0 units

F Write these numbers in tens and units:

☆ 20 2 tens 0 units

1 30
2 70
3 50
4 60
5 90
6 40
7 100
8 80
9 10

You can show numbers using **apparatus**:

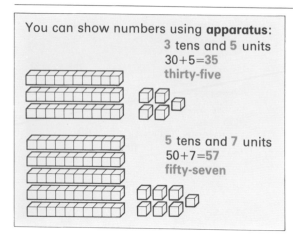

3 tens and 5 units
30+5=**35**
thirty-five

5 tens and 7 units
50+7=**57**
fifty-seven

A Write each number shown below in three different ways:

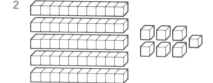

☆ 2 tens and 6 units
26
twenty-six

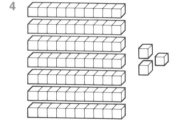

B Write in **words**. How many pencils?

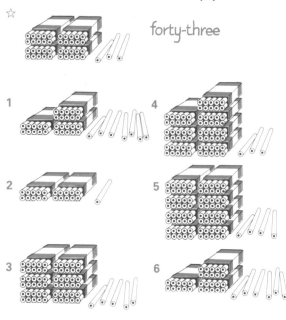

☆ forty-three

C Write in **figures**. How many sweets?

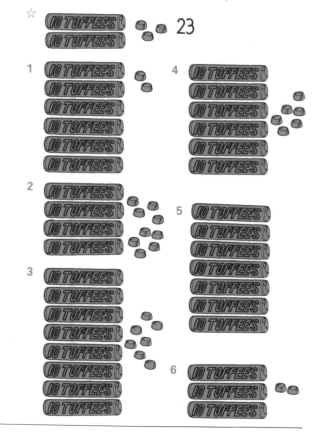

☆ 23

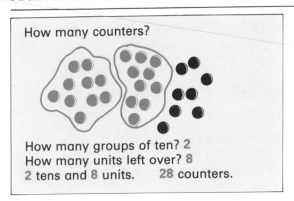

How many counters?

How many groups of ten? **2**
How many units left over? **8**
2 tens and **8** units.   **28** counters.

A Write how many counters in 2 different ways:

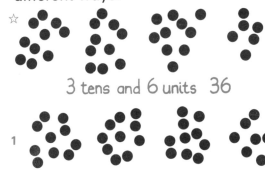

☆ 3 tens and 6 units 36

1

2

3

4

5

6

7

B Use counters if you need to.
How many groups of ten counters can you make with:

☆ 34 counters? 3

1	23 counters?	6	92 counters?
2	47 counters?	7	79 counters?
3	61 counters?	8	54 counters?
4	59 counters?	9	85 counters?
5	30 counters?	10	100 counters?

C Sweets are put in packs of 10.

How many left over with:

☆ 46 sweets? 6

1	21 sweets?	6	35 sweets?
2	54 sweets?	7	80 sweets?
3	17 sweets?	8	95 sweets?
4	36 sweets?	9	50 sweets?
5	62 sweets?	10	99 sweets?

D Write in figures:

☆ twenty-nine 29

1	twenty-six	6	ninety-four
2	fifty-one	7	eighty-seven
3	sixty-eight	8	thirty
4	forty-nine	9	sixty-four
5	seventeen	10	fifty-three

E Write these numbers as words:

☆ 37 thirty-seven

1	49	6	21	11	12
2	76	7	53	12	48
3	35	8	78	13	81
4	92	9	96	14	67
5	17	10	38	15	99

	UNITS									
	0	1	2	3	4	5	6	7	8	9
0	0	1	2	3	4	5	6	7	8	9
1	10	11	12	13	14	15	16	17	18	19
2	20	21	22	23	24	25	26	27	28	29
3	30	31	32	33	34	35	36	37	38	39
4	40	41	42	43	44	45	46	47	48	49
5	50	51	52	53	54	55	56	57	58	59
6	60	61	62	63	64	65	66	67	68	69
7	70	71	72	73	74	75	76	77	78	79
8	80	81	82	83	84	85	86	87	88	89
9	90	91	92	93	94	95	96	97	98	99
10	100									

(TENS down the left side)

A Write these numbers in **tens** and **units**:

☆ 46   4 tens 6 units

1 38   5 92   9 53
2 19   6 27   10 88
3 57   7 72   11 64
4 43   8 35   12 41

B Write the number that is:

☆ 6 tens and 3 units   63

1 3 tens and 2 units
2 9 tens and 7 units
3 2 tens and 0 units
4 7 tens and 7 units
5 0 tens and 5 units
6 6 tens and 8 units
7 8 tens and 6 units
8 5 tens and 1 unit
9 1 ten and 5 units
10 10 tens and 0 units
11 3 tens and 6 units
12 8 tens and 2 units

C Write numbers for *'s:

☆ 70+6=* 76

1 20+3=*   5 30+4=*
2 40+7=*   6 70+6=*
3 90+9=*   7 50+0=*
4 20+8=*   8 40+5=*

D Write the number that is **1 more than**:

☆ 37 38

1 24   4 90   7 19
2 65   5 69   8 88
3 19   6 10   9 59

E Write the number that is **1 less than**:

☆ 32 31

1 57   4 61   7 11
2 79   5 34   8 20
3 92   6 68   9 80

F Copy and complete:

☆ 26 * 28 * 30 * *
26 27 28 29 30 31 32

1 43 * * 46 * * * 50
2 28 * * * 32 * 34 *
3 79 * * 82 * * * 86
4 93 * 95 * * 98 * *
5 * 17 * * * * 22 *

G Write these numbers in order, **smallest first**:

☆ 43 26 84 52 90
26 43 52 84 90

1 35 79 14 50 22
2 96 75 92 70 87
3 63 36 60 30 66
4 19 91 22 99 11
5 10 100 1 11 0

Numbers to 100

place value: working in tens 27

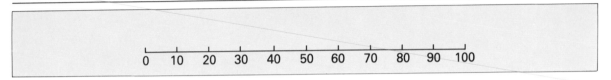

A Write numbers for ✱'s:

☆ 10 ✱ ✱ 40 ✱ ✱ 70
10 20 30 40 50 60 70

1 30 ✱ ✱ ✱ 70 ✱ 90
2 0 ✱ ✱ 30 ✱ ✱ 60
3 20 ✱ ✱ 50 ✱ 70 ✱
4 40 ✱ ✱ ✱ 80 90 ✱

B Write the number that is **10 less than**:

☆ seventy sixty

1 thirty   5 twenty
2 sixty   6 ninety
3 forty   7 fifty
4 eighty   8 one hundred

C Count in tens.
Copy and complete:

☆ 3 ✱ ✱ 33 ✱ ✱ 63
3 13 23 33 43 53 63

1 5 ✱ ✱ ✱ 45 ✱ 65
2 22 ✱ ✱ 52 ✱ ✱ 82
3 37 ✱ 57 ✱ ✱ 87 ✱
4 19 ✱ ✱ ✱ ✱ 69 79

D Count back in tens.
Copy and complete:

☆ 72 ✱ ✱ 42 ✱ ✱ 12
72 62 52 42 32 22 12

1 85 ✱ ✱ ✱ 45 ✱ 25
2 71 ✱ 51 ✱ ✱ 21 ✱
3 98 ✱ ✱ 68 ✱ ✱ 38
4 77 ✱ ✱ 47 ✱ ✱ 17

E How many **ten pence** are worth:

☆ 50p? 5
1 40p?   4 80p?   7 10p?
2 70p?   5 60p?   8 20p?
3 30p?   6 90p?

F How many tens?

☆ 4 tens+3 tens   ☆ 5 tens−2 tens
7 tens   3 tens

1 6 tens+3 tens   6 8 tens−4 tens
2 4 tens+2 tens   7 9 tens−5 tens
3 5 tens+4 tens   8 10 tens−5 tens
4 3 tens+5 tens   9 7 tens−5 tens
5 3 tens+3 tens   10 9 tens−8 tens

G Write numbers for ✱'s:

☆ 40+20=✱ 60
1 30+10=✱   6 40+40=✱
2 40+30=✱   7 30+40=✱
3 60+20=✱   8 20+70=✱
4 50+40=✱   9 30+50=✱
5 70+20=✱   10 50+50=✱

H How much money altogether if:

☆ John has 50p and is given 20p? 70p

1 Sharon is given 40p and then 30p more?
2 Anne is given 60p then another 30p?
3 Mike has 70p and is given 20p more?
4 Alan has 40p and is given 50p more?
5 Joy is given 30p and then another 40p?
6 Trevor has 50p and is given 20p more?
7 Dennis is given 20p then 60p more?

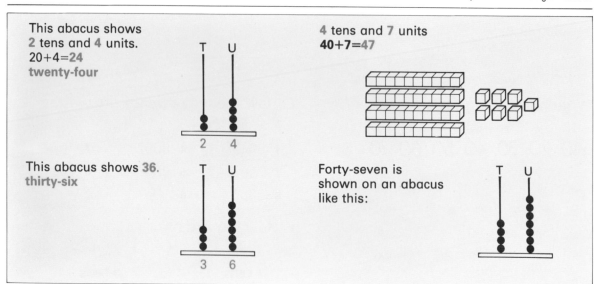

This abacus shows
2 tens and **4** units.
20+4=**24**
twenty-four

This abacus shows **36**.
thirty-six

4 tens and **7** units
40+7=47

Forty-seven is
shown on an abacus
like this:

A Write these abacus numbers in
2 different ways:

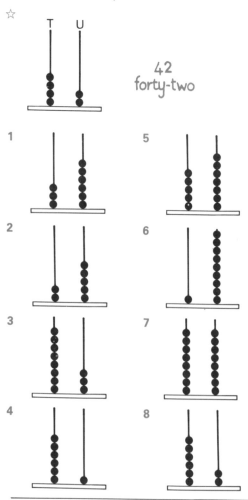

42
forty-two

1

2

3

4

5

6

7

8

B Draw an abacus picture to show
how many in each group:

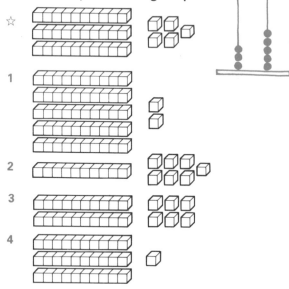

1

2

3

4

C Draw abacus pictures to show
these numbers:

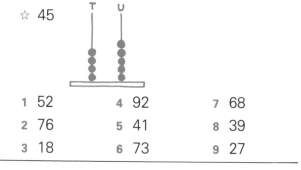

☆ 45

1 52   4 92   7 68

2 76   5 41   8 39

3 18   6 73   9 27

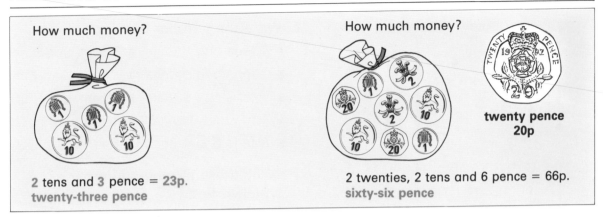

How much money?

2 tens and 3 pence = **23p**.
twenty-three pence

How much money?

twenty pence
20p

2 twenties, 2 tens and 6 pence = **66p**.
sixty-six pence

A Write how much money in 3 different ways:

B Write how much money in 2 different ways:

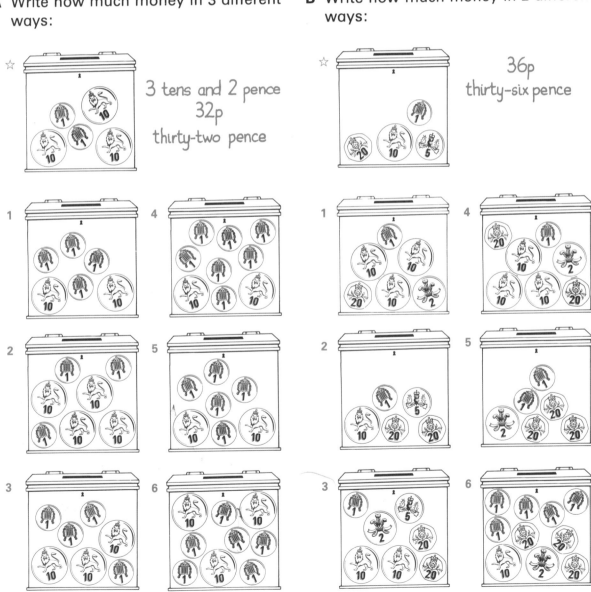

☆ 3 tens and 2 pence
32p
thirty-two pence

☆ 36p
thirty-six pence

A Write these abacus numbers:

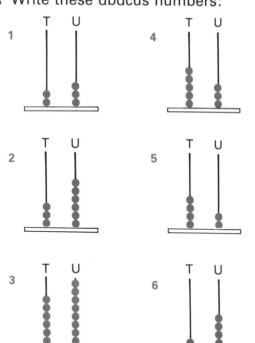

B Write in figures:

1 fifty-one
2 thirty-five
3 seventy-six
4 ninety-three
5 sixty-nine
6 eleven
7 twenty-eight
8 forty-two
9 eighty-seven
10 seventeen

C Write these numbers in words:

1 37
2 29
3 69
4 88
5 19
6 70
7 43
8 93
9 46
10 50
11 24
12 16

D How many groups of 10 counters can you make with:

1 27 counters?
2 35 counters?
3 51 counters?
4 93 counters?
5 89 counters?
6 64 counters?
7 72 counters?
8 47 counters?
9 16 counters?
10 26 counters?

E Write the number that is:

1 4 tens and 5 units
2 2 tens and 8 units
3 7 tens and 6 units
4 1 ten and 9 units
5 8 tens and 4 units
6 5 tens and 6 units
7 9 tens and 3 units
8 3 tens and 9 units
9 1 ten and 1 unit
10 6 tens and 5 units

F Write these numbers in order, **smallest first**:

1 26 17 39 41 60
2 92 71 17 63 35
3 30 16 13 62 90
4 27 72 36 63 13
5 87 88 78 77 79

G Add 10 to each of these numbers:

1 26
2 19
3 42
4 64
5 53
6 47
7 82
8 60
9 36
10 28
11 49
12 62

H How much money?

The Fishing game

16+4=

12+5=

5+9=

15−9=

8+7=

19−7=

10−4=

11+8=

15−7=

60+20=

Bob

Fred

Jane

Ann

Mike

Trevor

Ben

Alex

Beverley

Steve

Five people have
caught the right fish.
Write down their names.

A Which is the **shorter** fish, red or black?

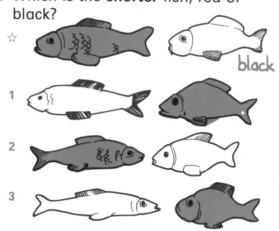

B Which is the **longer** rod, black or red?

red

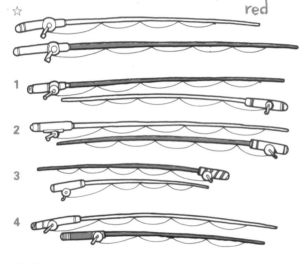

C Who is the **taller**?

Jim

D Which is the **narrower** glass, red or black?

black

E Which is the **thinner** string, red or black?

red

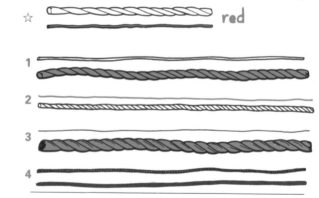

F 1 Is your pencil **longer** than this line?

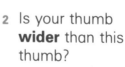

2 Is your thumb **wider** than this thumb?

3 Are you **shorter** than your teacher?

4 Is your pencil **narrower** than your thumb?

Length

Distances can be measured in **metres**.

A **metre rule** can be used for measuring distances:

The length of the bookcase is **greater than** 1 metre.

This door handle is about 1 metre from the floor.

A Are these measures greater than 1 metre or less than 1 metre?

☆ the **length** of an aeroplane

 greater

1 the **height** of your school

2 the **length** of a pin

3 the **height** of an elephant

4 the **length** of a key

5 the **length** of your arm

6 the **height** of your teacher

B Use a metre rule to answer these:

1 Is your classroom **more than** 8 metres long?

2 Is your desk **less than** 4 metres from the classroom door?

3 Are you **more than** 1 metre tall?

4 Is the classroom door **less than** 1 metre wide?

5 Is your teacher's desk **more than** 4 metres from your desk?

C Name 3 objects in your classroom that are:

1 **longer than** 1 metre

2 **shorter than** 1 metre

3 **about the same length as** 1 metre

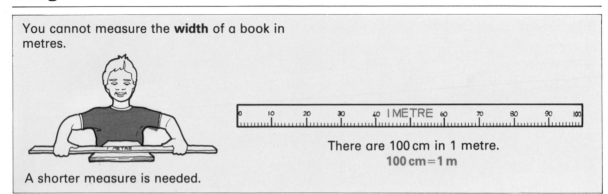

You cannot measure the **width** of a book in metres.

A shorter measure is needed.

There are 100 cm in 1 metre.

100 cm = 1 m

A Use a ruler to measure.
Write the lengths of these objects
in centimetres:

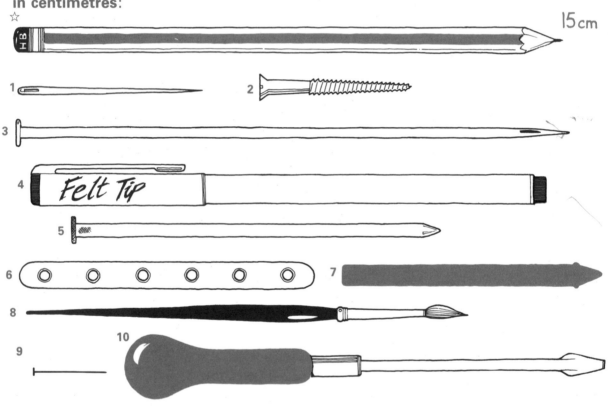

☆ 15 cm

1

2

3

4

5

6   7

8

10

9

B Write the lengths of these lines
in centimetres:

☆ —————————————— 6 cm

1 ————

2 ——————————

3 ——————

4 ——————————

5 ————————————

C Draw **straight lines** of these lengths:

☆ 5 cm ——————————

1 7 cm   6 11 cm

2 9 cm   7 14 cm

3 2 cm   8 6 cm

4 12 cm   9 10 cm

5 15 cm   10 8 cm

Length

The Great Snail Escape!

The Snailery

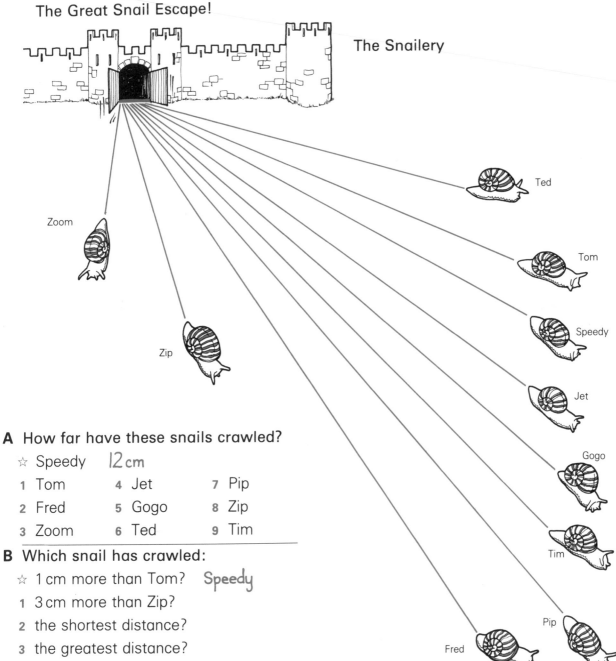

Zoom

Zip

Ted

Tom

Speedy

Jet

Gogo

Tim

Pip

Fred

A How far have these snails crawled?

☆ Speedy   12 cm

1 Tom   4 Jet   7 Pip
2 Fred   5 Gogo   8 Zip
3 Zoom   6 Ted   9 Tim

B Which snail has crawled:

☆ 1 cm more than Tom?   Speedy
1 3 cm more than Zip?
2 the shortest distance?
3 the greatest distance?
4 3 cm more than Gogo?
5 5 cm less than Tim?
6 6 cm less than Fred?
7 5 cm more than Jet?
8 less than 4 cm?
9 further than Fred?
10 3 cm further than Zoom?

C Which snails have crawled:

☆ less than 10 cm?   Ted, Zip, Zoom
1 more than 5 cm?
2 between 5 cm and 10 cm?
3 further than Ted?
4 less than 14 cm?

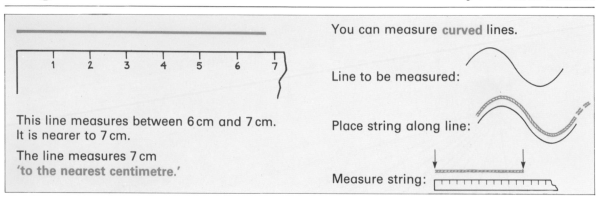

This line measures between 6 cm and 7 cm. It is nearer to 7 cm.

The line measures 7 cm 'to the nearest centimetre.'

You can measure **curved** lines.

Line to be measured:

Place string along line:

Measure string:

A Measure these lines to the nearest centimetre:

☆ 4 cm

1

2

3

4

5

6

7

8

B Measure these lines to the nearest centimetre. Which is **longer**, red or black?

☆ red

1

2

3

4

5

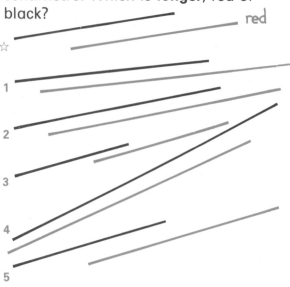

C Use string to measure. Measure each snake **to the nearest centimetre**:

1 Which is the longest snake?

2 Which is the shortest snake?

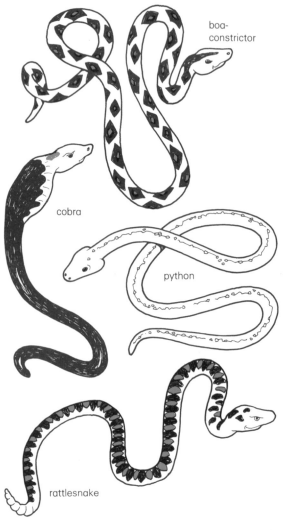

boa-constrictor

cobra

python

rattlesnake

Weight

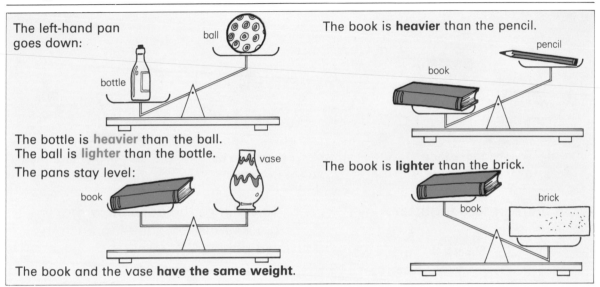

The left-hand pan goes down:

The bottle is **heavier** than the ball.
The ball is **lighter** than the bottle.
The pans stay level:

The book and the vase **have the same weight**.

The book is **heavier** than the pencil.

The book is **lighter** than the brick.

A Which object is **lighter**?

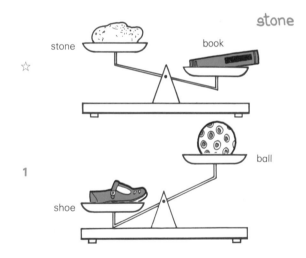

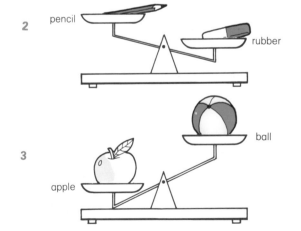

B Name 5 things in the classroom that you think are **heavier** than this book.
☆ blackboard

C Name 5 things in the classroom that you think are **lighter** than this book.
☆ crayon

D 1 Name 3 objects that you think are **about the same weight as** this book.

2 Use scales or a balance. Put the book on one pan. Put the objects one at a time on the other pan.

3 Copy and complete this table:

name of object	heavier or lighter than book

E Name 3 things that are lighter than your pencil.
☆ fly

F Name 3 things that are heavier than an elephant.
☆ jumbo jet

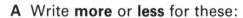

The cup weighs **more than** 4 blocks.

The cup weighs **the same as** 5 blocks.

The cup weighs **less than** 6 blocks.

A Write **more** or **less** for these:

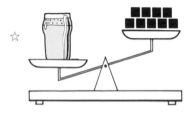

☆ Does the glass weigh more or less than 9 blocks?

more

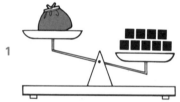

1 Does the purse weigh more or less than 9 blocks?

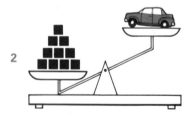

2 Does the car weigh more or less than 10 blocks?

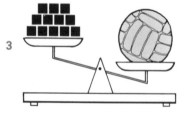

3 Does the ball weigh more or less than 12 blocks?

4 Does the doll weigh more or less than 13 blocks?

B To balance the pans, how many blocks must be added to each **red** pan?

3

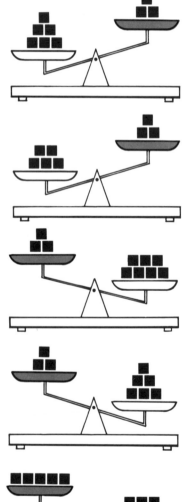

☆

1

2

3

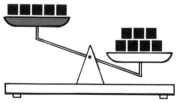

4

Weight

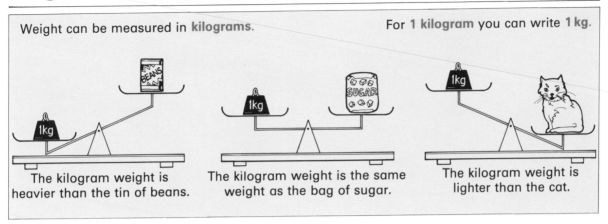

Weight can be measured in **kilograms**.

For **1 kilogram** you can write **1 kg**.

The kilogram weight is heavier than the tin of beans.

The kilogram weight is the same weight as the bag of sugar.

The kilogram weight is lighter than the cat.

A Are these objects heavier or lighter than 1 kilogram?

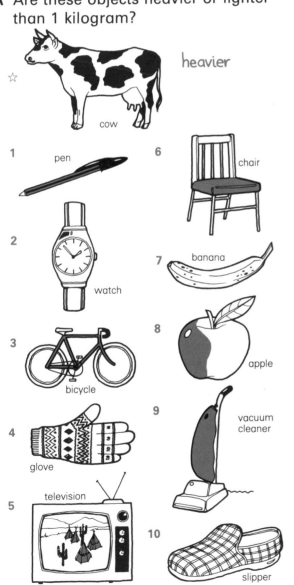

☆ cow — heavier

1 pen

2 watch

3 bicycle

4 glove

5 television

6 chair

7 banana

8 apple

9 vacuum cleaner

10 slipper

B Look at the objects below:

dustbin, motorbike, horse, hairbrush, scissors, fork, nail, rose, toothbrush, car, table, man, dog, ruler

heavier than 1 kg	lighter than 1 kg
☆ man	nail

1 Copy the table above.
2 List seven objects that are **heavier** than 1 kg.
3 List seven objects that are **lighter** than 1 kg.

The bottle holds more than the glass.

The bottle has the greater **capacity**.

Capacity can be measured in **litres**.

This mug holds less than 1 litre.

This bottle holds about 1 litre.

This bucket holds more than 1 litre.

A Which object has the greater **capacity**?

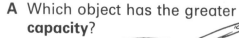

cup   saucepan   *saucepan*

1

mug   jug

2

cup   glass

3

spoon   mug

4

bowl   bath

5
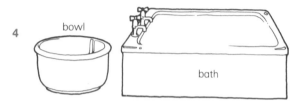

bottle   saucepan

B Is the capacity of each container greater or less than **1 litre**? *greater*

swimming pool

1 bath

6 glass

2 egg cup

7 fish tank

3 barrel

8 bowl

4 thimble

9 cup

5 dustbin

10 watering can

A Write **red** or **black**:

1 Which is the longer line?

2 Which is the narrower thumb?

3 Which is the wider string?

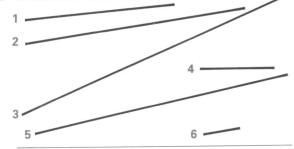

B Measure these lines in centimetres:

1
2
3
4
5
6

C Draw lines of these lengths:

1 6 cm   5 10 cm
2 9 cm   6 5 cm
3 2 cm   7 3 cm
4 11 cm 8 12 cm

D Measure these lines to the **nearest** centimetre:

1
2
3
4
5
6

E Which object is **heavier**?

1 glass, cup
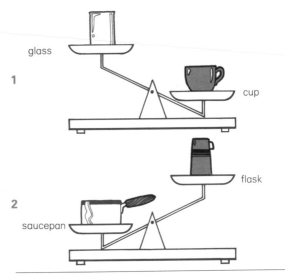

2 saucepan, flask

F Do these objects weigh more than 1 kilogram, or less than 1 kilogram?

1
2

G Which object has the greater capacity?

1 cup   thimble

2 spoon   glass

3 jam jar   egg cup

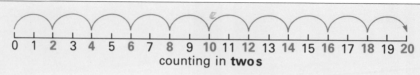

counting in **twos**

A Count in **twos**.
Copy and complete:

☆ 4 ∗ ∗ 10 ∗ ∗ 16

    4   6   8 10 12 14 16

1 0 ∗ 4 6 ∗ 10 12

2 6 ∗ 10 ∗ 14 ∗ 18

3 2 4 ∗ 8 ∗ ∗ 14

4 10 ∗ ∗ 16 ∗ 20 22

5 14 ∗ ∗ ∗ 22 24 ∗

6 20 ∗ ∗ ∗ ∗ ∗ 32

B Use a hundred square.
Finish colouring squares by counting in **twos**:

1	2	3	4	5	6	7	8	9	10
11	12	13	14	15	16	17	18	19	20
21	22	23	24	25	26	27	28	29	30
31	32	33	34	35	36	37	38	39	40
41	42	43	44	45	46	47	48	49	50
51	52	53	54	55	56	57	58	59	60
61	62	63	64	65	66	67	68	69	70
71	72	73	74	75	76	77	78	79	80
81	82	83	84	85	86	87	88	89	90
91	92	93	94	95	96	97	98	99	100

C Copy and complete:

1 The coloured numbers in my square are called e — — n numbers.

2 The numbers that are not coloured are called o — — numbers.

D Are these numbers **even** or **odd**?

☆ 21   odd

1 6

2 9

3 5

4 1

5 12

6 17

7 23

8 28

9 30

10 29

11 43

12 55

13 82

14 69

15 54

16 77

17 89

18 96

E Count in **twos**. Work out:

☆ How many wheels?   6

1 How many ears?

2 How many legs?

3 How many shoes?

4 How many feet?

5 How many hands?

For **2+2+2** write: **2×3**
Say: '2 **multiplied by 3**'

For **2+2+2+2** write: **2×4**
Say: '2 **multiplied by 4**'

For **2×3=6** say:
'**2 multiplied by 3 equals 6**'

For **2×4=8** say:
'**2 multiplied by 4 equals 8**'

A Copy and complete:

☆	2+2+2+2+2+2	2×6	12
1	2+2+2		
2	2+2+2+2+2		
3		2×4	
4	2+2		
5	2+2+2+2+2+2+2+2		16
6	2+2+2+2+2+2+2+2+2		
7		2×7	
8	2+2+2+2+2+2+2+2+2		

B Copy and complete:

☆	2×1=2	2 multiplied by 1 equals 2
1	2×2=4	
2	2×3=✳	
3	2×4=✳	
4		2 multiplied by 5 equals 10
5	2×6=12	
6	2×7=✳	
7		2 multiplied by 8 equals ✳
8	2×9=✳	
9	2×10=✳	

C **Multiply** to answer these:

☆ How many ears? 2×4=8

1 How many eyes?

2 How many wings?

3 How many wheels?

4 How many dots?

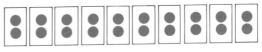

D **Multiply** to answer these:

☆ How many arms on 6 children? 2×6=12
1 How many ears on 4 cats?
2 How many feet on 10 ducks?
3 How many legs on 7 geese?
4 How many wings on 5 birds?
5 How many eyes on 9 dolls?
6 How many feet on 2 birds?
7 How many ears on 8 tigers?
8 How many arms on 3 people?

E Write numbers for ✳'s:

☆ 2×2=✳ 4

1 2×5=✳   4 2×3=✳   7 2×4=✳
2 2×7=✳   5 2×10=✳ 8 2×6=✳
3 2×1=✳   6 2×9=✳   9 2×8=✳

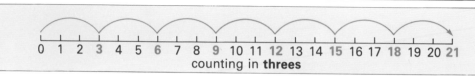
counting in **threes**

A Count in **threes**.
Copy and complete:

☆ 6 ✳ 12 ✳ 18 ✳ 24
  6 9 12 15 18 21 24
1 0 ✳ 6 9 ✳ 15 18
2 3 ✳ 9 ✳ 15 ✳ 21
3 12 ✳ 18 ✳ 24 ✳ 30
4 18 ✳ ✳ 27 ✳ ✳ 36
5 9 ✳ ✳ ✳ ✳ ✳ 27

For **3+3** write: **3×2**.
Say: '3 multiplied by 2'

For **3+3+3+3** write: **3×4**
Say: '3 multiplied by 4'

For **3×2=6** say:
'3 multiplied by 2 equals 6'

For **3×4=12** say:
'3 multiplied by 4 equals 12'

B Count in **threes**.
Work out how many:

☆ wheels?
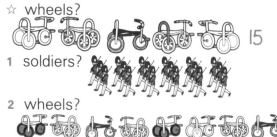
15

1 soldiers?

2 wheels?

3 dots?

C Use a hundred square.
Finish colouring squares by counting in threes:

1	2	3	4	5	6	7	8	9	10
11	12	13	14	15	16	17	18	19	20
21	22	23	24	25	26	27	28	29	30
31	32	33	34	35	36	37	38	39	40
41	42	43	44	45	46	47	48	49	50
51	52	53	54	55	56	57	58	59	60
61	62	63	64	65	66	67	68	69	70
71	72	73	74	75	76	77	78	79	80
81	82	83	84	85	86	87	88	89	90
91	92	93	94	95	96	97	98	99	100

D Copy and complete:

☆	3+3+3+3	3×4	3 multiplied by 4=12
1	3+3+3+3+3+3		
2		3×10	
3			3 multiplied by 3=9
4		3×8	
5	3+3+3+3+3		
6		3×9	
7			3 multiplied by 7=21

E **Multiply** to answer these.
How many wheels on:

☆ 6 tricycles? 3×6=18
1 8 tricycles?   5 7 tricycles?
2 10 tricycles?   6 3 tricycles?
3 2 tricycles?   7 5 tricycles?
4 9 tricycles?   8 11 tricycles?

F Write numbers for ✳'s:

☆ 3×5=✳ 15
1 3×6=✳   5 3×10=✳
2 3×2=✳   6 3×9=✳
3 3×7=✳   7 3×3=✳
4 3×1=✳   8 3×8=✳

Multiplication

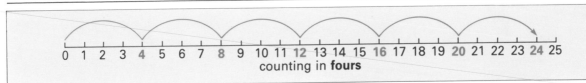

counting in **fours**

A Count in **fours**.
Copy and complete:

☆ 8 ✳ 16 ✳ 24 ✳ 32
  8 12 16 20 24 28 32

1 0 ✳ 8 ✳ 16 ✳ 24

2 12 ✳ 20 24 ✳ 32 ✳

3 4 ✳ 12 ✳ 20 ✳ 28

4 16 ✳ ✳ 28 ✳ ✳ 40

5 20 ✳ ✳ ✳ ✳ ✳ 44

B Use a hundred square.
Finish colouring squares by counting in **fours**:

1	2	3	4	5	6	7	8	9	10
11	12	13	14	15	16	17	18	19	20
21	22	23	24	25	26	27	28	29	30
31	32	33	34	35	36	37	38	39	40
41	42	43	44	45	46	47	48	49	50
51	52	53	54	55	56	57	58	59	60
61	62	63	64	65	66	67	68	69	70
71	72	73	74	75	76	77	78	79	80
81	82	83	84	85	86	87	88	89	90
91	92	93	94	95	96	97	98	99	100

C Count in **fours**.
Work out how many:

☆ wheels?

 20

1 legs?

2 legs?

3 legs?

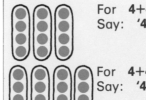

For **4+4+4** write: **4×3**
Say: **'4 multiplied by 3'**

For **4+4+4+4** write: **4×4**
Say: **'4 multiplied by 4'**

For **4×3=12** say:
'4 multiplied by 3 equals 12'

For **4×4=16** say:
'4 multiplied by 4 equals 16'

D **Multiply** to find how many holes:

☆ $4 \times 5 = 20$

1

2

3

4

E **Multiply** to answer these.
How many legs on:

☆ 6 lions? $4 \times 6 = 24$

1 5 deer?   6 4 camels?

2 3 cats?   7 8 sheep?

3 2 dogs?   8 11 cows?

4 7 tigers?   9 9 horses?

5 10 elephants? 10 12 goats?

F Write numbers for ✳'s:

☆ $4 \times 1 = $ ✳   4

1 $4 \times 5 = $ ✳   6 $4 \times 6 = $ ✳

2 $4 \times 7 = $ ✳   7 $4 \times 10 = $ ✳

3 $4 \times 4 = $ ✳   8 $4 \times 3 = $ ✳

4 $4 \times 8 = $ ✳   9 $4 \times 9 = $ ✳

5 $4 \times 2 = $ ✳   10 $4 \times 11 = $ ✳

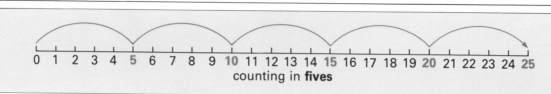

counting in **fives**

A Count in **fives**.
Copy and complete:

☆ 10 ＊ 20 ＊ 30 ＊ 40
   10 15 20 25 30 35 40

1 0 ＊ 10 ＊ 20 ＊ 30
2 15 ＊ 25 ＊ 35 ＊ 45
3 5 ＊ 15 ＊ ＊ 30 35
4 20 ＊ ＊ 35 ＊ ＊ 50
5 35 ＊ ＊ ＊ ＊ ＊ 65

B Use a hundred square.
Finish colouring squares by counting in **fives**:

1	2	3	4	5	6	7	8	9	10
11	12	13	14	15	16	17	18	19	20
21	22	23	24	25	26	27	28	29	30
31	32	33	34	35	36	37	38	39	40
41	42	43	44	45	46	47	48	49	50
51	52	53	54	55	56	57	58	59	60
61	62	63	64	65	66	67	68	69	70
71	72	73	74	75	76	77	78	79	80
81	82	83	84	85	86	87	88	89	90
91	92	93	94	95	96	97	98	99	100

C Count in **fives**.
Work out how many toes:

☆   20
1
2
3
4
5

For **5+5** write: **5×2**
Say: **'5 multiplied by 2'**

For **5+5+5+5** write: **5×4**
Say: **'5 multiplied by 4'**

For **5×2=10** say:
'5 multiplied by 2 equals 10'

For **5×4=20** say:
'5 multiplied by 4 equals 20'

D **Multiply** to find how many legs:

☆ $5 \times 3 = 15$
1
2
3

E **Multiply** to answer these:

☆ How many legs on 4 starfish? $5 \times 4 = 20$
1 How many toes on 7 feet?
2 How many legs on 3 starfish?
3 How many toes on 10 feet?
4 How many legs on 8 starfish?
5 How many toes on 5 feet?

F Write numbers for ＊'s:

☆ $5 \times 6 =$ ＊   30

1 $5 \times 2 =$ ＊   6 $5 \times 8 =$ ＊
2 $5 \times 5 =$ ＊   7 $5 \times 1 =$ ＊
3 $5 \times 10 =$ ＊   8 $5 \times 11 =$ ＊
4 $5 \times 7 =$ ＊   9 $5 \times 3 =$ ＊
5 $5 \times 4 =$ ＊   10 $5 \times 9 =$ ＊

Multiplication

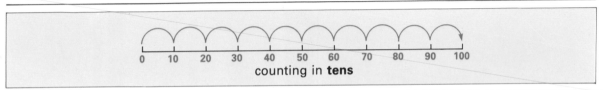
counting in **tens**

A Count in **tens**. Copy and complete:

☆ 20   ✳   ✳   50   ✳   ✳   80

   20 30 40 50 60 70 80

1   0   ✳   20   30   40   ✳   60

2   30   ✳   50   ✳   70   ✳   90

3   10   ✳   30   ✳   ✳   60   ✳

4   40   ✳   ✳   70   ✳   ✳   100

10 + 10 + 10 + 10 = 40

10×4=40. Say:

'10 multiplied by 4 equals 40'

B Use a hundred square. Finish colouring squares by counting in **tens**:

1	2	3	4	5	6	7	8	9	10
11	12	13	14	15	16	17	18	19	20
21	22	23	24	25	26	27	28	29	30
31	32	33	34	35	36	37	38	39	40
41	42	43	44	45	46	47	48	49	50
51	52	53	54	55	56	57	58	59	60
61	62	63	64	65	66	67	68	69	70
71	72	73	74	75	76	77	78	79	80
81	82	83	84	85	86	87	88	89	90
91	92	93	94	95	96	97	98	99	100

C Count in **tens**.
Work out how many pencils:

☆ 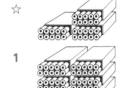 30

1 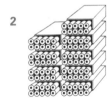   3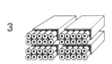

2   4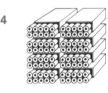

D Multiply to find how many toes:

☆  10×4=40

1

2

E Multiply to find how many pence:

☆  10×5=50

1

2

3

F Write numbers for ✳'s:

☆ 10×3=✳   30

1   10×6=✳   4   10×7=✳   7   10×10=✳

2   10×4=✳   5   10×9=✳   8   10×2=✳

3   10×1=✳   6   10×5=✳   9   10×8=✳

A How many each if:

☆ the spiders catch an equal number of flies? 3

1 each man has the same number of dogs?

2 the dogs catch an equal number of cats?

3 the men have an equal number of birds?

4 each man has the same number of cats?

5 the birds eat an equal number of worms?

6 the cats catch an equal number of mice?

B How many each if you:

☆ share the flies equally among 6 spiders? 2

1 share the worms equally among 6 birds?

2 share the cats equally among 4 men?

3 share the mice equally among 3 cats?

4 share the flies equally among 3 spiders?

5 share the birds equally among 3 men?

6 share the worms equally among 2 birds?

C How many each if you:

☆ share these dummies equally among 3 babies? 2

1 share these sweets equally among 4 children?

2 share these coins equally between 2 children?

3 share these balls equally between 5 children?

4 share these carrots equally among 3 rabbits?

5 share these coins equally among 3 children?

Division

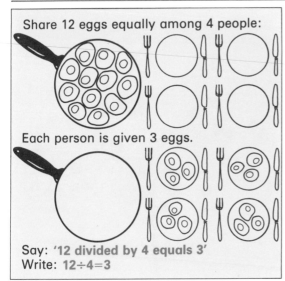

Share 12 eggs equally among 4 people:

Each person is given 3 eggs.

Say: '12 divided by 4 equals 3'
Write: 12÷4=3

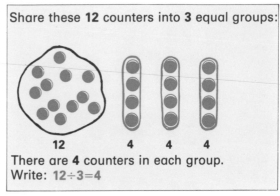

Share these **12** counters into **3** equal groups:

12   4   4   4

There are **4** counters in each group.
Write: 12÷3=4

A Write these answers in 2 different ways:

☆ Share 10 sausages equally between 2 children:
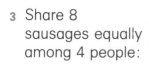
10 divided by 2 = 5
10÷2=5
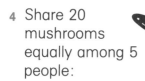

1 Share 15 eggs equally among 5 people:

2 Share 12 pieces of bacon equally among 3 people:

3 Share 8 sausages equally among 4 people:

4 Share 20 mushrooms equally among 5 people:

B Use counters if you need to. Share these counters into:

☆ 2 equal groups   8÷2=4

1 3 equal groups

2 2 equal groups

3 4 equal groups

4 5 equal groups

5 3 equal groups

6 10 equal groups

C Use counters if you need to. Copy and complete:

☆ 6÷2=✶   6÷2=3

1 10÷2=✶   4 18÷3=✶   7 16÷4=✶

2 8÷4=✶   5 20÷10=✶   8 25÷5=✶

3 10÷5=✶   6 21÷3=✶   9 20÷4=✶

Apples are packed in **fours**.
How many packs can be made from
12 apples?

After 1 pack is made, **8 apples** are left:

After 2 packs are made, **4 apples** are left:

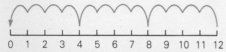

After 3 packs are made, **no apples** are left!

0 1 2 3 4 5 6 7 8 9 10 11 12

3 groups of 4 can be subtracted from 12.
3 packs can be made.

How many groups of **3** can you
make from these counters:

15 counters

0 1 2 3 4 5 6 7 8 9 10 11 12 13 14 15

5 groups of 3 can be subtracted from 15.
5 groups can be made.

A Find how many packs
can be made when:

☆ these apples are packed in **threes**:

 5

1 these apples are packed in **twos**:

2 these tomatoes are packed in **fives**:

3 these oranges are packed in **fours**:

4 these plums are packed in **threes**:

5 these onions are packed in **twos**:

B Use counters if you need to.
Find how many groups
can be made when:

☆ these counters are in groups of 4:

 3 groups

1 these counters are in groups of 2:

2 these counters are in groups of 3:

3 these counters are in groups of 5:

4 these counters are in groups of 4:

5 these counters are in groups of 10:

6 these counters are in groups of 5:

Division

How many groups of **2** can you make from **10**?

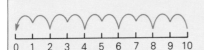

0 1 2 3 4 5 6 7 8 9 10

5 groups of 2 can be subtracted from 10.
5 groups can be made.
Say: **'10 divided by 2 equals 5'**
Write: **10÷2=5**

How many groups of 5 can you make from 15?

0 1 2 3 4 5 6 7 8 9 10 11 12 13 14 15

15÷5=3
3 groups can be made.

A Use a number line if you need to.

☆ How many groups of 2 can be made from 8? $8÷2=4$ 4 groups

1 How many groups of 2 can be made from 12?

2 How many groups of 3 can be made from 18?

3 How many groups of 4 can be made from 20?

4 How many groups of 5 can be made from 25?

5 How many groups of 10 can be made from 30?

6 How many groups of 4 can be made from 28?

7 How many groups of 3 can be made from 27?

8 How many groups of 2 can be made from 20?

B Use division to answer these:

☆ Apples are packed in fours. How many packs can be made with 20 apples? $20÷4=5$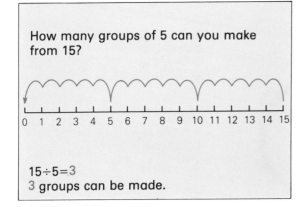
5 packs

1 Onions are packed in threes. How many packs can be made with 21 onions?

2 Bananas are sold in bunches of 4. How many bunches can be made with 40 bananas?

3 Sweets cost 2p each. How many can you buy with 20p?

4 Balls are packed in tens. How many packs can be made with 70 balls?

5 Lollies cost 10p. How many lollies can you buy with 90p?

6 Felt pens are packed in fives. How many packs can be made with 35 pens?

7 Oranges are packed in threes. How many packs can be made with 30 oranges?

8 Pencils cost 5p. How many pencils can you buy with 45p?

C Use a number line if you need to. Write numbers for ✶'s:

☆ $20÷4=$✶   5

1 $16÷2=$✶
2 $18÷3=$✶
3 $15÷5=$✶
4 $24÷4=$✶
5 $30÷10=$✶

6 $25÷5=$✶
7 $40÷10=$✶
8 $50÷10=$✶
9 $32÷4=$✶
10 $100÷10=$✶

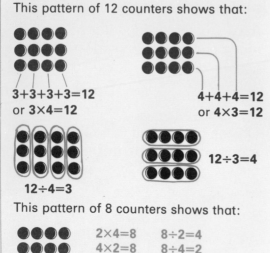

This pattern of 12 counters shows that:

3+3+3+3=12
or 3×4=12

4+4+4=12
or 4×3=12

12÷4=3

12÷3=4

This pattern of 8 counters shows that:

2×4=8   8÷2=4
4×2=8   8÷4=2

If you know that 3×5=15
you can write 3 more facts:

5×3=15
15÷3=5
15÷5=3

A Write numbers for ✳'s:

☆ 3×2=✳ 6
  2×3=✳ 6
  6÷2=✳ 3
  6÷✳=2 3

1 5×3=✳
   3×5=✳
   15÷3=✳
   15÷5=✳

2 4×5=✳
   5×✳=20
   20÷✳=5
   20÷✳=4

3 4×2=✳
   2×4=✳
   8÷4=✳
   8÷✳=4

4 2×10=✳
   10×✳=20
   20÷✳=10
   20÷✳=2

5 3×3=✳
   ✳÷3=3

B Write 3 more facts for each of these:

☆ 5×2=10   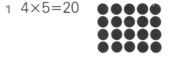 2×5=10
                              10÷2=5
                              10÷5=2

1 4×5=20

2 5×3=15

3 20÷2=10

4 18÷3=6

C Use counters if you need to.
  Write numbers for ✳'s:

☆ 5×4=20
  4×5=✳   20
  20÷✳=5   4
  20÷✳=4   5

1 2×6=12
   6×2=✳
   ✳÷2=6
   ✳÷6=2

2 4×3=12
   3×✳=12
   12÷✳=3
   ✳÷3=4

3 10×3=30
   3×✳=30
   ✳÷10=3
   30÷✳=10

4 10×5=50
   5×✳=50
   50÷✳=5
   50÷✳=10

Revision for pages 42–52

A Are these numbers even or odd?

1	17	6	14	11	40
2	24	7	11	12	107
3	32	8	3	13	65
4	60	9	99	14	112
5	71	10	66	15	200

B Copy and complete:

1	4+4+4+4+4	4×5	
2		3×7	21
3	5+5+5+5+5		25
4		2×8	
5	10+10+10+10+10+10+10		
6		5×7	
7		10×6	
8		2×9	
9	3+3+3+3+3+3+3+3		
10		5×9	
11		4×7	
12	4+4+4+4+4+4+4+4		

C Write numbers for *'s:

1 2×7= *
2 4×6= *
3 3×8= *
4 10×9= *
5 2×9= *
6 4×4= *
7 3×9= *
8 2×11= *
9 4×8= *
10 3×7= *
11 5×5= *
12 3×10= *
13 10×5= *
14 2×6= *
15 4×9= *
16 5×9= *
17 3×6= *
18 4×7= *
19 5×8= *
20 2×5= *
21 10×10= *
22 4×11= *
23 5×7= *
24 3×3= *

D How many each when:

1 24 fish are divided equally among 3 fishermen?
2 27 sweets are divided equally among 3 children?
3 50 worms are shared equally among 5 birds?
4 18 flies are shared equally between 2 spiders?

E How many packs when:

1 18 apples are packed in twos?
2 27 apples are packed in threes?
3 40 apples are packed in fours?
4 100 apples are packed in tens?
5 45 apples are packed in fives?
6 24 apples are packed in threes?
7 36 apples are packed in fours?

F Write numbers for *'s:

1 12÷2= *
2 20÷2= *
3 15÷3= *
4 27÷3= *
5 40÷4= *
6 16÷4= *
7 25÷5= *
8 40÷5= *
9 60÷10= *
10 40÷10= *
11 16÷2= *
12 6÷3= *
13 18÷3= *
14 28÷4= *
15 36÷4= *
16 100÷10= *

G Write numbers for *'s:

1 3×5= *
2 5×3= *
3 15÷5= *
4 15÷3= *
5 4×10= *
6 10×4= *
7 40÷10= *
8 40÷4= *
9 4×5= *
10 5×4= *
11 20÷5= *
12 20÷4= *

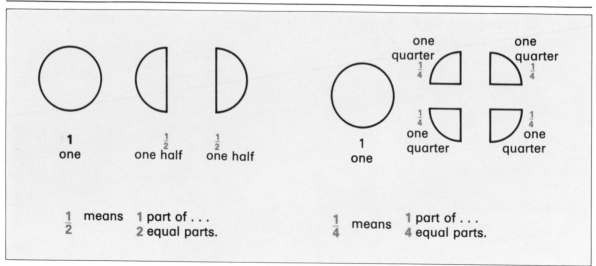

$\frac{1}{2}$ means 1 part of . . . 2 equal parts.

$\frac{1}{4}$ means 1 part of . . . 4 equal parts.

A Copy these shapes on squared paper. Colour $\frac{1}{2}$ of each shape:

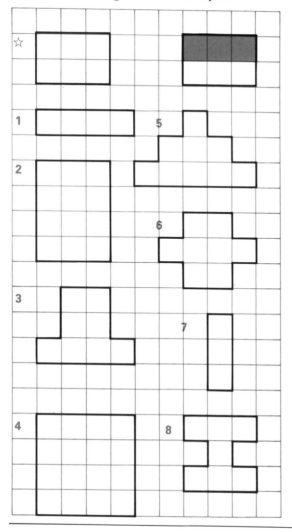

B Copy these shapes on squared paper. Colour $\frac{1}{4}$ of each shape:

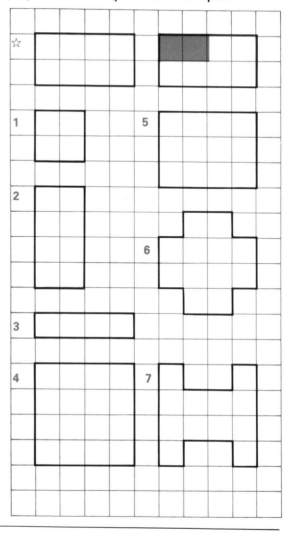

Fractions

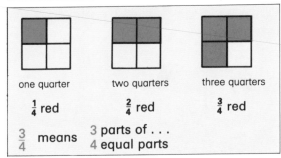

one quarter — $\frac{1}{4}$ red

two quarters — $\frac{2}{4}$ red

three quarters — $\frac{3}{4}$ red

$\frac{3}{4}$ means 3 parts of . . . 4 equal parts

A What **fraction** of each shape is red?

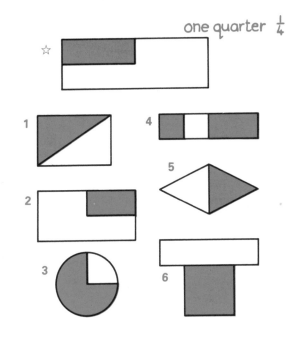

one quarter $\frac{1}{4}$

☆

1

2

3

4

5

6

C What fraction of each shape is **black**, and what fraction is **red**?

☆

black $\frac{1}{4}$ red $\frac{1}{2}$

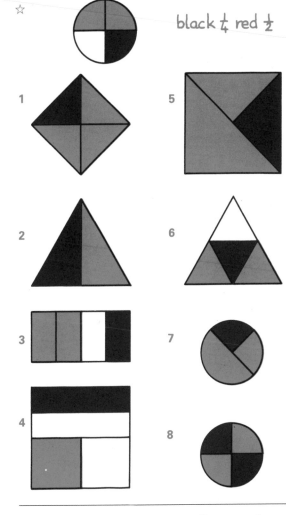

1

2

3

4

5

6

7

8

B Copy these on squared paper. Colour the fraction shown:

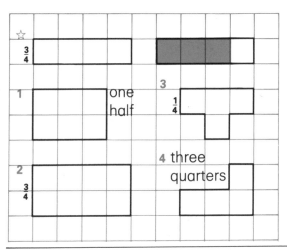

☆ $\frac{3}{4}$

1 one half

3 $\frac{1}{4}$

2 $\frac{3}{4}$

4 three quarters

D How many whole oranges will give:

☆ 6 halves? 3

1 10 halves?

2 12 halves?

3 4 quarters?

4 16 halves?

5 20 halves?

6 8 quarters?

7 12 quarters?

8 2 halves?

9 16 quarters?

10 40 halves?

The long hand is the **minute** hand.
The short hand is the **hour** hand.

The time on this clock is 5 o'clock.

A Write these times:

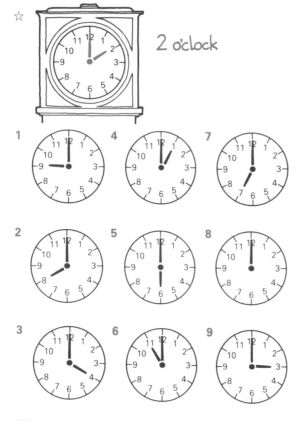

☆ 2 o'clock

C Write the time that is 1 hour **later** than:

☆ 6 o'clock

1   3   5

2   4   6

D Write the time that is 1 hour **earlier** than:

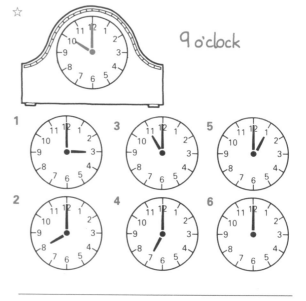

☆ 9 o'clock

1   3   5

2   4   6

B Use clock faces to show these times.

☆ 10 o'clock:

1	1 o'clock	4	11 o'clock	7	3 o'clock
2	7 o'clock	5	6 o'clock	8	5 o'clock
3	9 o'clock	6	8 o'clock	9	12 o'clock

E What do you think you will be doing tomorrow morning at:

☆ 2 o'clock? sleeping

1	10 o'clock?	4	8 o'clock?
2	6 o'clock?	5	5 o'clock?
3	9 o'clock?	6	11 o'clock?

Time

The **minute** hand is half way round.

The **hour** hand is between the 8 and the 9.

The time on this clock is **half past 8**.

The time on this clock is **half past four**.

Half an hour **earlier** the time was **four o'clock**:

Half an hour **later** the time will be **five o'clock**.

A Write these times:

half past four

1

4

7

2

5

8

3

6

9

B Draw clock faces to show these times:

☆ half past 2

1 half past 8

2 half past 11

3 half past 6

4 half past 1

5 half past 5

6 half past 9

7 half past 10

8 half past 12

9 half past 3

C Use a clock face if you need to. Write the time that is half an hour **earlier** than:

9 o'clock

1

2

3

D Write the time that is half an hour **later** than:

6 o'clock

1

3

5

2

4

6

The **minute** hand is one quarter way round.

The **hour** hand is just past the 10.

The time on this clock is: $\frac{1}{4}$ **past ten**.

 The time on this clock is **quarter past seven**.

$\frac{1}{4}$ of an hour **earlier** the time was **seven o'clock**:

 $\frac{1}{4}$ of an hour **later** the time will be **half past seven**.

A Write these times:

 $\frac{1}{4}$ past 5

1  **4** **7**

2 **5** **8**

3 **6** **9**

B Use clock faces to show these times:

☆ $\frac{1}{4}$ past 8

1 $\frac{1}{4}$ past 7   4 $\frac{1}{4}$ past 4   7 $\frac{1}{4}$ past 2
2 $\frac{1}{4}$ past 6   5 $\frac{1}{4}$ past 1   8 $\frac{1}{4}$ past 11
3 $\frac{1}{4}$ past 3   6 $\frac{1}{4}$ past 10   9 $\frac{1}{4}$ past 12

C Use a clock face if you need to. Write the time that is $\frac{1}{4}$ hour **earlier** than:

☆ 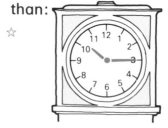 10 o'clock

1  **3** **5**

2  **4** **6**

D Write the time that is $\frac{1}{4}$ hour **later** than:

☆  half past one

1  **2** **3**

Time

The minute hand still has a quarter to turn.
The hour hand is nearly on the 3.

The time on this clock is **quarter to three.**

The time on this clock is **quarter to five.**

$\frac{1}{4}$ of an hour **earlier** the time was half past four:

$\frac{1}{4}$ of an hour **later** the time will be five o'clock.

A Write these times:

 quarter to six

1 **4** **7**

2  **5** **8**

3  **6** **9**

B Use clock faces to show these times:

☆ $\frac{1}{4}$ to 7

1 $\frac{1}{4}$ to 8　**4** $\frac{1}{4}$ to 6　**7** $\frac{1}{4}$ to 3

2 $\frac{1}{4}$ to 10　**5** $\frac{1}{4}$ to 1　**8** $\frac{1}{4}$ to 5

3 $\frac{1}{4}$ to 12　**6** $\frac{1}{4}$ to 9　**9** $\frac{1}{4}$ to 11

C Use a clock face if you need to.
Write the time that is $\frac{1}{4}$ hour **earlier** than:

☆ half past one

1 **2** **3**

D Write the time that is $\frac{1}{4}$ hour **later** than:

 11 o'clock

1 **3** **5**

2  **4** **6**

You need 12 clock faces stamped in your book.
Draw hands on your clock faces to show each of these times for Jimmy:

1 Wakes up	5 Starts maths lesson	9 Leaves school

half past seven   half past nine   four o'clock

2 Washes	6 Told off by teacher	10 Goes to play with friend

quarter to eight   quarter to eleven   quarter to five

3 Eats breakfast	7 Falls over in playground	11 Told off by mum

quarter past eight   quarter past twelve   half past six

4 Arrives at school	8 Starts lunch	12 Goes to bed

quarter to nine   half past twelve   eight o'clock

A What fraction of each shape is red?

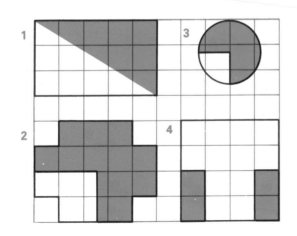

B How many whole apples will give:

1 4 halves?
2 8 halves?
3 4 quarters?
4 10 halves?
5 12 quarters?
6 16 halves?
7 16 quarters?
8 20 halves?
9 14 halves?
10 8 quarters?

C Write these times:

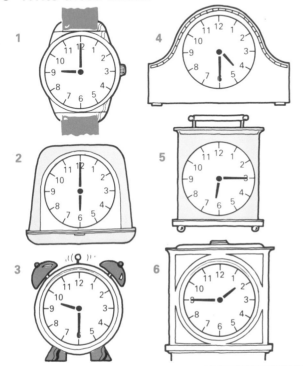

D Use clock faces to show these times:

1 7 o'clock
2 3 o'clock
3 10 o'clock
4 $\frac{1}{2}$ past four
5 $\frac{1}{2}$ past eleven
6 $\frac{1}{4}$ past nine
7 $\frac{1}{4}$ past two
8 $\frac{1}{4}$ to ten
9 $\frac{1}{4}$ to twelve
10 $\frac{1}{4}$ past six

E Write the time that is 1 hour earlier than:

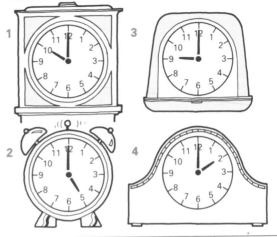

F Write the time that is half an hour later than:

G Write the time that is $\frac{1}{4}$ hour earlier than:

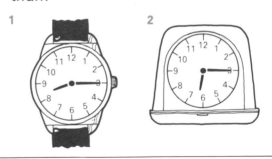

Here is a line of 6 counters: ●●●●●●
Here is a line of 4 counters: ●●●●

There are **2 more** counters on the top line.
The difference between the lines
is 2 counters.
You can use subtraction to
find the difference.

Write: **6−4=2**

A What is the **difference** between these
lines of counters?

☆ ●●●●●●●
  ●●●   4 counters

1 ●●●●●●●●
  ●●●●●●

2 ●●●●●●●
  ●●●●●●

3 ●●●●●●●●●
  ●●●●●

4 ●●●●●●●●●●●●
  ●●●●●●

5 ●●●●●●●●
  ●●●●

6 ●●●●●●●●●●●●●
  ●●●●

7 ●●●●●●●●●●
  ●●

B Use counters if you need to.
Work out the **difference** between:

☆ 5 and 9   ●●●●●
           ●●●●●●●●●   4

1 6 and 8   5 3 and 10
2 3 and 7   6 2 and 11
3 2 and 8   7 6 and 12
4 4 and 9   8 4 and 12

C Use subtraction to find how many
more **black** counters than **red**
counters:

10−6=4

1   4
2   5
3   6

D Use subtraction to find the **difference**
between:

☆ 5 and 11   11−5=6
1 2 and 8   5 11 and 4   9 2 and 10
2 4 and 9   6 6 and 13   10 1 and 14
3 12 and 5   7 15 and 6   11 3 and 17
4 9 and 7   8 13 and 8   12 5 and 20

E Use subtraction to find how many
years **difference** in age if:

☆ John is 9 and Ann is 7   9−7=2
1 Bill is 10 and Jane is 6
2 Paula is 11 and Bob is 5
3 Jo is 9 and Jill is 2
4 Fred is 6 and Mike is 12
5 Alan is 7 and his brother is 18
6 Jess is 5 and her sister is 15
7 Anna is 8 and Sarah is 10
8 Trevor is 4 and Sue is 17
9 Joan is 19 and Max is 10
10 Sally is 6 and Lisa is 11

Difference

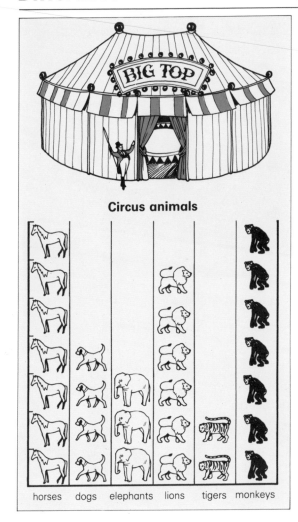

Circus animals

horses dogs elephants lions tigers monkeys

A Use the graph to find how many:

☆ dogs 4

1 elephants   3 horses   5 tigers

2 lions   4 monkeys

B Use the graph to answer these:

☆ How many more lions than dogs? 2

1 How many more horses than elephants?

2 How many more monkeys than lions?

3 How many more lions than tigers?

4 How many more monkeys than dogs?

5 How many animals altogether?

C Copy and complete this **picture graph** for John's pets:

John's pets

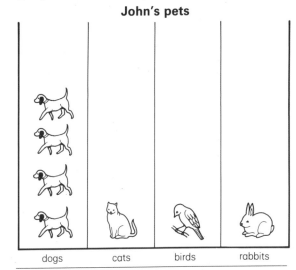

dogs   cats   birds   rabbits

D Use your **picture graph** to answer these:

☆ How many more birds than cats? 3

1 How many more dogs than cats?

2 How many more birds than dogs?

3 How many more rabbits than cats?

4 How many pets altogether?

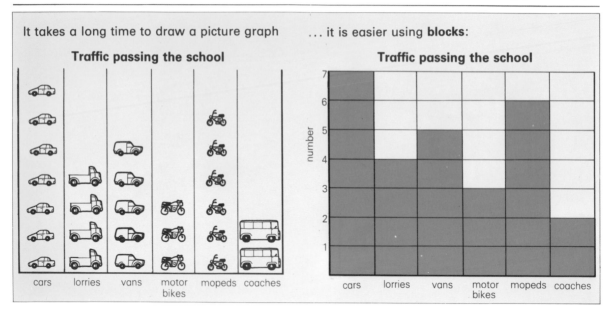

It takes a long time to draw a picture graph ... it is easier using **blocks**:

Traffic passing the school

Traffic passing the school

A Use the **block graph** to answer these:

☆ How many vans went past? 5

1 How many lorries went past?

2 How many coaches went past?

3 How many motorbikes went past?

4 How many cars went past?

5 How many mopeds went past?

6 How many more cars than lorries?

7 How many more vans than motorbikes?

8 How many more mopeds than lorries?

9 How many more cars than coaches?

10 How many more mopeds than motorbikes?

11 How many mopeds and motorbikes altogether?

12 How many coaches and lorries altogether?

13 How many cars and vans altogether?

14 How many fewer coaches than lorries?

15 How many fewer vans than cars?

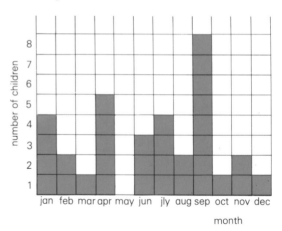

Birthday months for children in Class 3

B How many children had birthdays in:

☆ July? 4

1 April?   4 June?   7 November?

2 December?   5 March?   8 January?

3 February?   6 October?   9 May?

C Use the **block graph** to answer these.

1 Which month had most birthdays?

2 Which month had fewest birthdays?

3 How many birthdays altogether in January, February, March and April?

4 How many children in Class 3?

Difference

A The children in Class 3 were asked to name their favourite fruits.
This table shows their answers:

favourite fruit	apple	orange	banana	pear	plum
number of children	8	6	4	7	8

Copy and complete this block graph:

Favourite fruits of children in Class 3

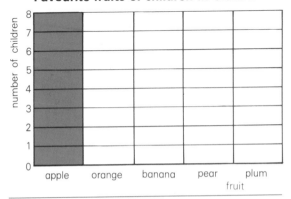

Colours of cars in Bill's garage

What is the **difference** between the number of black cars and the number of white cars?

   8 black cars
   2 white cars $8-2=6$
The difference in number is **6**.

B The children in Class 3 were asked to name their favourite colours.
This table shows their answers:

favourite colour	red	blue	green	yellow	orange	purple
number of children	6	5	2	7	1	7

Copy and complete this block graph:

Favourite colours of children in Class 3.

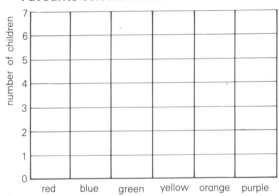

C What is the difference between:

☆ the number of yellow cars and the number of blue cars? $11-1=10$

1 the number of green cars and the number of brown cars?

2 the number of yellow cars and the number of orange cars?

3 the number of black cars and the number of blue cars?

4 the number of yellow cars and the number of green cars?

5 the number of orange cars and the number of white cars?

6 the number of yellow cars and the number of black cars?

7 the number of green cars and the number of red cars?

8 the number of black cars and the number of brown cars?

Sharon **estimated** (guessed) that the length of this line was 5 cm.
Then she **measured** the line. She found it was 7 cm long.

estimate: **5** cm   measure: **7** cm

The difference between the estimate and the measure was **7 cm − 5 cm = 2 cm**

A Copy this table. Do not fill it in yet:

spider	estimate	measure	difference
1	cm	cm	cm
2	cm	cm	cm
3	cm	cm	cm
4	cm	cm	cm
5	cm	cm	cm
6	cm	cm	cm
7	cm	cm	cm
8	cm	cm	cm
9	cm	cm	cm
10	cm	cm	cm

B 1 Estimate how far spider 1 has dropped. Write your estimate in the table.

2 Measure how far spider 1 has dropped. Write your measure in the table.

3 Work out the difference between your estimate and the measure. Write your answer in the table.

4 Do the same for the other spiders.

Difference

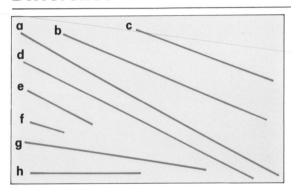

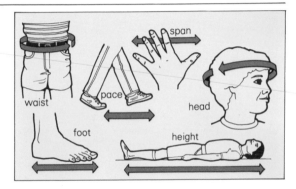

A Copy this table. Do not fill it in yet:

line	estimate	measure	difference
a	cm	cm	cm
b	cm	cm	cm
c	cm	cm	cm
d	cm	cm	cm
e	cm	cm	cm
f	cm	cm	cm
g	cm	cm	cm
h	cm	cm	cm

E Copy and complete this table:

distance	estimate	measure	difference
Your span	cm	cm	cm
Length of your foot	cm	cm	cm
Your pace	cm	cm	cm
Around your head	cm	cm	cm
Your height	cm	cm	cm
Around your waist	cm	cm	cm

B 1 Estimate the length of line **a**.

2 Measure the length of line **a**.

3 Work out the difference between your estimate and the measure.

4 Write your answers in the table.

5 Do the same for the other lines.

C How long altogether?

☆ line **d**+line **e** $7\text{cm} + 2\text{cm} = 9\text{cm}$

1 line **a**+line **g**   4 line **a**+line **b**+line **d**

2 line **b**+line **h**   5 line **d**+line **g**+line **h**

3 line **c**+line **d**   6 line **a**+line **c**+line **h**

D What is the **difference** in length between these lines?

☆ line **b** and line **g** $6\text{cm} - 5\text{cm} = 1\text{cm}$

1 line **b** and line **e**   4 line **e** and line **g**

2 line **f** and line **h**   5 line **h** and line **c**

3 line **d** and line **f**   6 line **c** and line **f**

F

1 Write who you think is taller, the policeman or the burglar.

2 Measure each person. Were you right?

When you count coins, count the highest values first:

fifty pence
50p

50 ...70 ...80 ...85 ...87 ...88 pence.

A How much money in each box?

☆

50...60...70...75...77..78 pence

1

2

3

4

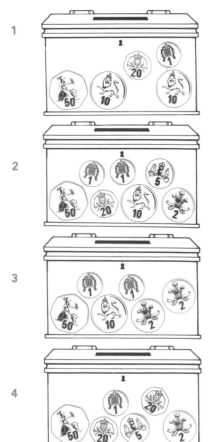

B Write words for ✱'s.
One 50p coin has the same value as:

☆ ✱10p coins five

1 ✱1p coins   3 ✱ 2p coins

2 ✱ 5p coins

C

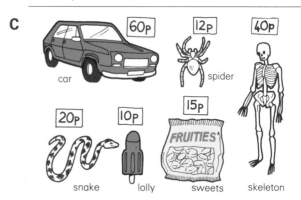

60p car
12p spider
40p skeleton
20p snake
10p lolly
15p sweets FRUITIES

How much do you pay for:

☆ a skeleton and sweets? 40p+15p=55p

1 a car and a snake?

2 a lolly and a spider?

3 two snakes?

4 two lollies?

5 a snake and sweets?

D Which two coins will **exactly** pay for these?

☆ a spider 10p and 2p

1 a car   4 a lolly

2 a snake   5 a bag of sweets

3 a skeleton

Money

You can pay **exactly** for this car using these coins:

72p

Here is the way to pay **exactly** using the **fewest** coins:

A Write a set of coins that will pay **exactly** for these:

☆ a soldier
27p

10p, 5p, 5p, 2p, 2p, 2p, 1p.

1 a monkey
45p

4 a gun
63p

2 a flying saucer
86p

5 a ship
57p

3 a doll
94p

6 a teddy bear
99p

B Which two coins will pay **exactly** for these?

☆

BOOK of the WORLD
40p
20p, 20p.

1 ball
60p

4 cow
30p

2 pencil
11p

5 skipping rope
70p

3 lorry
55p

6 balloon
12p

C Write the fewest coins to pay **exactly** for:

☆ trick ink blot 72p
50p, 20p, 2p.

1 robot 48p

5 picture 99p

2 mug 62p

6 book 80p
BOOK of WORMS

3 bat 88p

7 sweets 55p
SWEETS

4 pen 75p

8 whistle 95p

D Write three coins to pay **exactly** for:

☆ cucumber 40p
20p, 10p, 10p.

1 apple
8p

5 orange
15p

2 carrots
26p

6 grapes
65p

3 melon
52p

7 pineapple
90p

4 onion
4p

8 grapefruit
16p

John buys a sweet for 6p.
He gives 10p to pay for it.
6p and **4p** make 10p.
He is given **4p** change.

Paula buys a cake for 34p.
She gives 50p to pay for it.
The baker gives change
using the fewest coins:

He says: '34 ...35 ...40 ...50'.
34p and **16p** make 50p.
Paula is given **16p change**.

A Write the missing amounts of money:

☆ Sally buys a chew for 3p.
She gives 5p to pay for it.
3p and ✱ make 5p.   2p
She is given ✱ change.   2p

1 Bill buys a bun for 7p.
He gives 10p to pay for it.
7p and ✱ make 10p.
He is given ✱ change.

2 Alan buys a sweet for 2p.
He gives 5p to pay for it.
2p and ✱ make 5p.
He is given ✱ change.

3 Jane buys a pencil for 5p.
She gives 10p to pay for it.
5p and ✱ make 10p.
She is given ✱ change.

4 Sue buys a flower for 14p.
She gives 20p to pay for it.
14p and ✱ make 20p.
She is given ✱ change.

B Copy and complete:

	cost	money given	change
☆	6p	10p	4p
1	3p	10p	
2	2p	5p	
3	18p	20p	
4	13p	20p	

C Write the coins that are added to these amounts to make 50p:

☆ 27p   27   ...28   ...30   ...50
        1p, 2p, 20p.

1 35p   35   ...40   ...50

2 29p   29   ...30   ...50

3 31p   31   ...33   ...35   ...40   ...50

4 24p   24   ...25   ...30   ...50

5 42p   42   ...43   ...45   ...50

D Use coins if you need to.
How much **change** from 50p when you spend:

☆ 32p?   18p

1 46p?   5 36p?   9 22p?

2 44p?   6 30p?   10 19p?

3 40p?   7 25p?   11 16p?

4 39p?   8 28p?   12 11p?

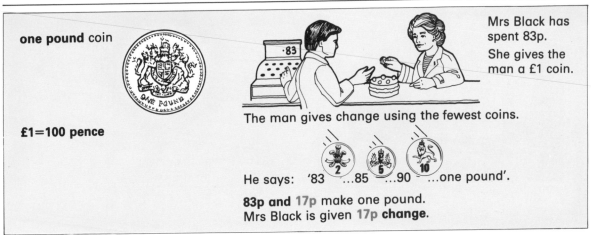

one pound coin

£1=100 pence

Mrs Black has spent 83p.
She gives the man a £1 coin.

The man gives change using the fewest coins.

He says: '83 ...85 ...90 ...one pound'.

83p and **17p** make one pound.
Mrs Black is given **17p change**.

A Write words for ✳'s.
£1 has the same value as:

☆ ✳ 10p coins   ten

1 ✳ 50p coins   4 ✳ 1p coins

2 ✳ 5p coins   5 ✳ 2p coins

3 ✳ 20p coins

B There is £1 in each of these boxes.
What is the hidden coin?

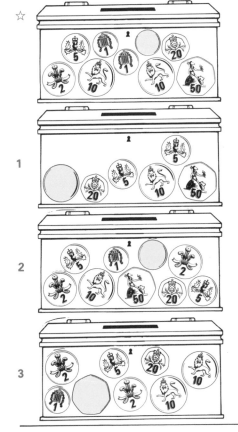

☆   1p

C Write the coins added to these amounts to make £1:

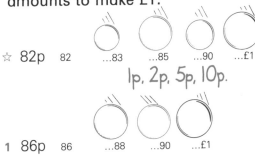

☆ 82p 82 ...83 ...85 ...90 ...£1

1p, 2p, 5p, 10p.

1 86p 86 ...88 ...90 ...£1

2 73p 73 ...75 ...80 ...£1

3 68p 68 ...70 ...80 ...£1

4 57p 57 ...58 ...60 ...80 ...£1

D Use coins if you need to.
How much **change** from £1 when you spend:

☆ 54p? 46p

1 68p?   5 48p?   9 19p?

2 92p?   6 37p?   10 23p?

3 85p?   7 30p?   11 26p?

4 59p?   8 44p?   12 11p?

Animals on the farm

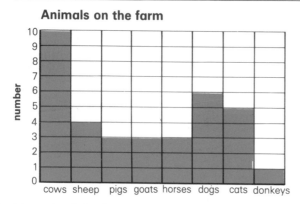

A Use the block graph to answer these:

1 How many sheep?

2 How many cows?

3 How many animals altogether?

4 How many more dogs than donkeys?

5 How many more cats than goats?

6 What is the difference between the number of pigs and the number of horses?

7 What is the difference between the number of cats and the number of cows?

8 What is the difference between the number of dogs and the number of goats?

B Copy and complete the table:

1 ——————— 2 ———————

3 ———————

4 —— 5 ———————

6 ———————

line	estimate	measure	difference
1	cm	cm	cm
2	cm	cm	cm
3	cm	cm	cm
4	cm	cm	cm
5	cm	cm	cm
6	cm	cm	cm

C How much money in each box?

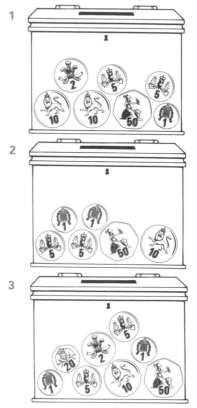

1

2

3

D Which 3 coins will exactly pay for these?

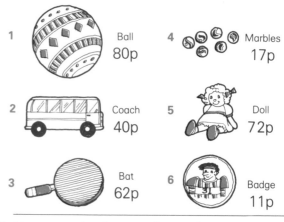

1 Ball 80p

2 Coach 40p

3 Bat 62p

4 Marbles 17p

5 Doll 72p

6 Badge 11p

E How much change from £1 when you spend:

1 75p? 4 59p? 7 32p?

2 86p? 5 52p? 8 25p?

3 63p? 6 71p? 9 18p?

Shape

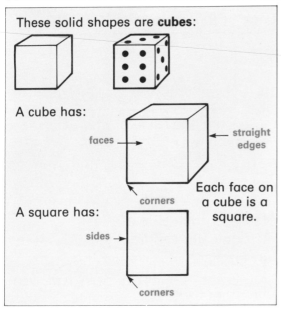

These solid shapes are **cubes**:

A cube has:

faces →
← straight edges

corners

Each face on a cube is a square.

A square has:

sides →

corners

A Use a cube if you need to.

1 How many faces on a cube?

2 How many straight edges on a cube?

3 How many corners on a cube?

4 How many sides on a square?

5 How many corners on a square?

B You need some squared paper.

Make a pattern of squares on your paper.

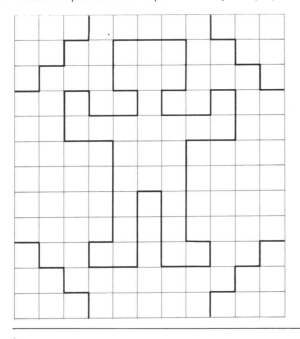

C

1 Measure each side of this square in centimetres.

2 Are all 4 sides the same length?

D Part of the square is hidden. Write the length of each side:

☆

2 cm, 2 cm, 2 cm, 2 cm

1

2

3

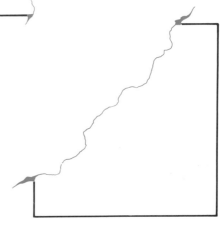

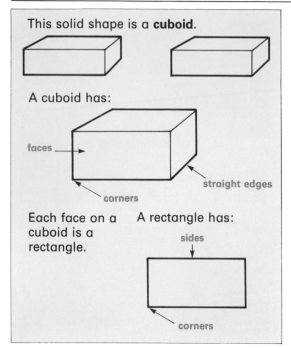

This solid shape is a **cuboid**.

A cuboid has:

faces

straight edges

corners

Each face on a cuboid is a rectangle.

A rectangle has:

sides

corners

A Use a cuboid if you need to:

1 How many faces on a cuboid?
2 How many straight edges on a cuboid?
3 How many corners on a cuboid?
4 How many sides on a rectangle?
5 How many corners on a rectangle?

B Here are some useful cuboids:

Name ten other useful cuboids.

☆ tea packet

C Look at this rectangle:

1 Measure each side of the rectangle in centimetres.
2 How many sides measure 5 cm?
3 How many sides measure 2 cm?

D Measure each side of these rectangles in centimetres:

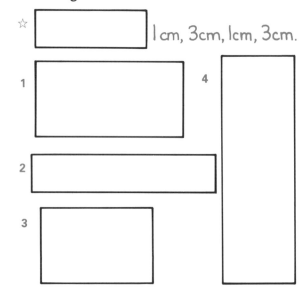

☆ 1cm, 3cm, 1cm, 3cm.

E Part of the rectangle is hidden. Write the length of each side:

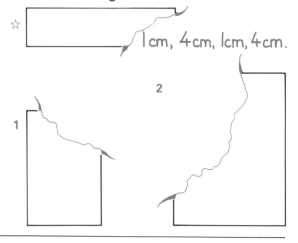

☆ 1cm, 4cm, 1cm, 4cm.

Shape

This solid shape is a **triangular prism**:

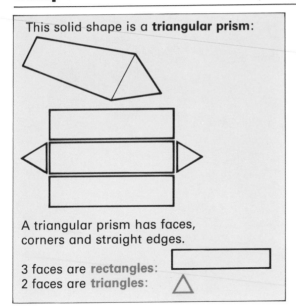

A triangular prism has faces, corners and straight edges.

3 faces are **rectangles**:
2 faces are **triangles**:

A Use a triangular prism if you need to.

1 How many faces on a triangular prism?

2 How many straight edges on a triangular prism?

3 How many corners on a triangular prism?

4 How many sides on a triangle?

5 How many corners on a triangle?

B Where would you see these triangular prisms?

☆ on a house

1 TOBLERONE

2

3

4

C Triangles can be seen in many places:

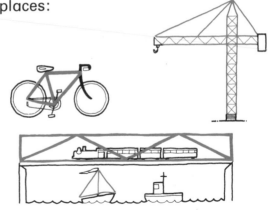

Draw five other pictures that show triangles.

D Write the name of each shape:

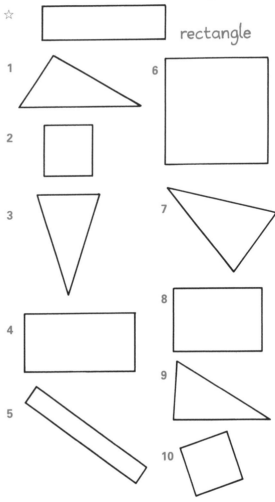

☆ rectangle

1

2

3

4

5

6

7

8

9

10

A Write 15 things in the picture that turn.

☆  doorhandle

B Write 5 things in the picture that **can** make a **full** turn.

☆  wheel

C Write 5 things in the picture that **cannot** make a **full** turn.

☆  door

Turns can be made:

clockwise or **anti-clockwise**.

D What are you facing if you:

☆ face the door, and then *make 1 full turn clockwise?* the door

1 face the teacher's desk, and then *make 1 full turn anti-clockwise?*

2 face the door, and then *make ½ turn clockwise?*

3 face the light switch, and then *make ½ turn anti-clockwise?*

4 face the door, and then *make ¼ turn anti-clockwise?*

5 face the teacher's desk, and then *make ¼ turn clockwise?*

Angles

These strips show different amounts of turn:

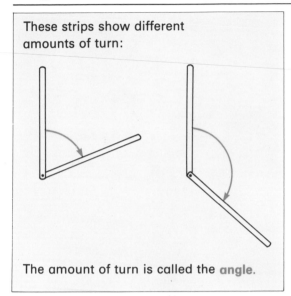

The amount of turn is called the **angle**.

This angle shows a square corner. It is called a **right angle**.

Right angles are shown like this:

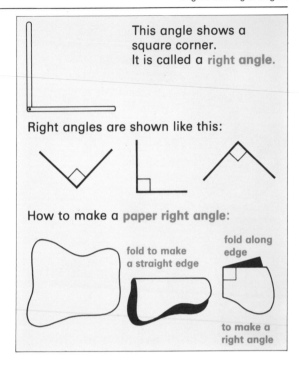

How to make a **paper right angle**:

fold to make a straight edge

fold along edge

to make a right angle

A Which is the larger angle?
Write **black** or **red**:

☆ black

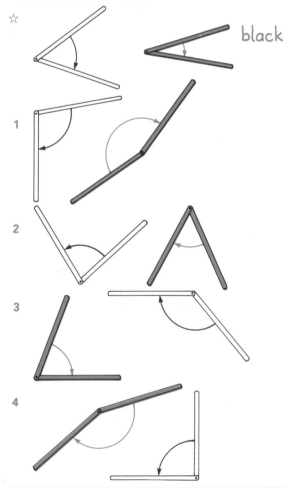

1

2

3

4

B Make a paper right angle.
See pictures above.

C Use your paper right angle.
Are these angles right angles?

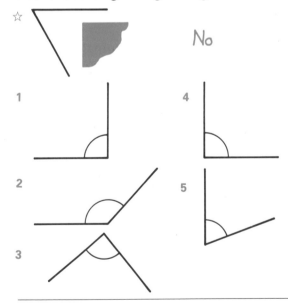

☆ No

1

4

2

5

3

D Use your paper right angle to find 20 right angles in your classroom.

☆ corner of the window frame

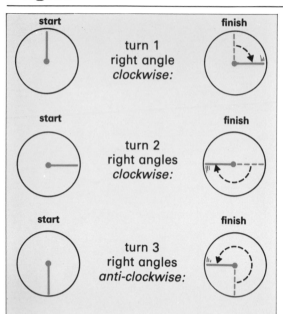

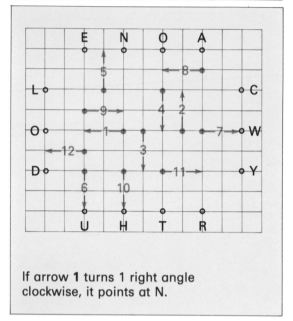

If arrow **1** turns 1 right angle clockwise, it points at N.

A Where will the arrow be after the turn?

☆ turn 2 right angles
clockwise

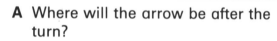

1 turn 1 right angle
anti-clockwise

4 turn 1 right angle
anti-clockwise

2 turn 2 right angles
anti-clockwise

5 turn 3 right angles
clockwise

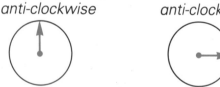

3 turn 3 right angles
clockwise

6 turn 3 right angles
anti-clockwise

B At which letter will arrow 3 point when it turns:

☆ 1 right angle anti-clockwise?   W

1 1 right angle clockwise?

2 3 right angles anti-clockwise?

3 3 right angles clockwise?

C Write down a letter for each ✳.
Find a secret message:

arrow	turn	letter
☆ 1	1 right angle anti-clockwise	H
2	1 right angle anti-clockwise	✳
3	3 right angles clockwise	✳
4	2 right angles anti-clockwise	✳
5	1 right angle anti-clockwise	✳
6	3 right angles anti-clockwise	✳
7	3 right angles clockwise	✳
8	3 right angles clockwise	✳
9	1 right angle anti-clockwise	✳
10	3 right angles clockwise	✳
11	1 right angle anti-clockwise	✳
12	3 right angles clockwise	✳

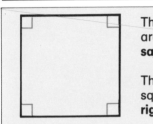

The **sides** of a square are all the **same length**.

The **angles** in a square are all **right angles**.

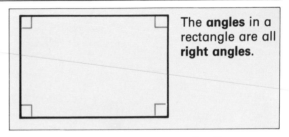

The **angles** in a rectangle are all **right angles**.

A Are these shapes squares?
Write **yes** or **no**:

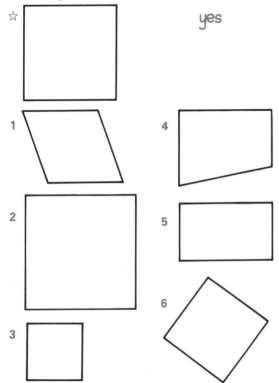

☆ yes

B Why are these shapes **not** squares?

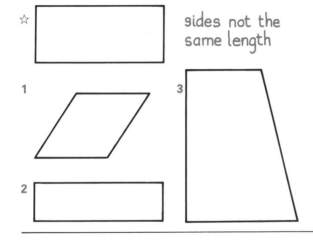

☆ sides not the same length

C Are these shapes rectangles?
Write **yes** or **no**:

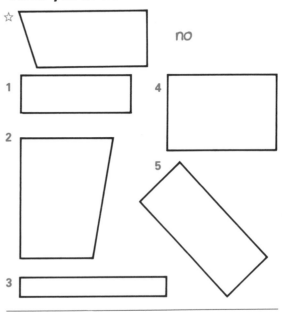

☆ no

D Are the two **red** sides of these rectangles the same length?

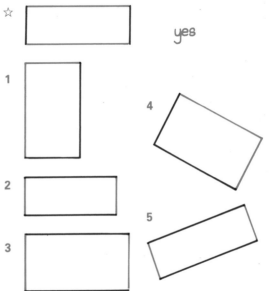

☆ yes

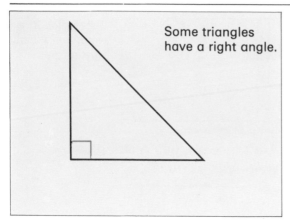

Some triangles have a right angle.

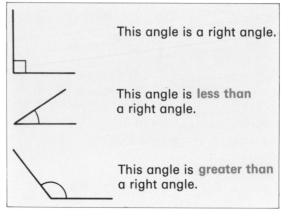

This angle is a right angle.

This angle is **less than** a right angle.

This angle is **greater than** a right angle.

A You will need a paper right angle.
Do these triangles have right angles?
Write **yes** or **no**:

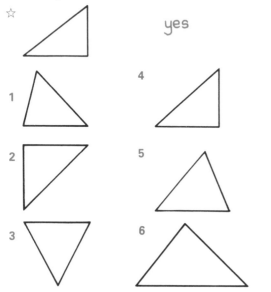

☆ yes

1

2

3

4

5

6

C Are these angles right angles?
If not, are they greater or less than right angles?

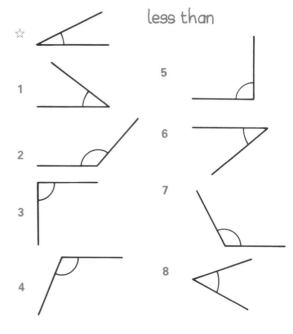

☆ less than

1

2

3

4

5

6

7

8

B Copy these triangles on squared paper. Mark the right angles:

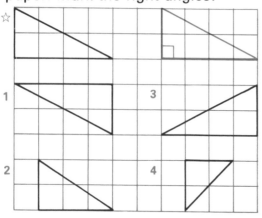

☆

1

2

3

4

D How many angles in these shapes are right angles?

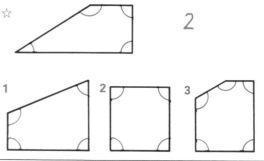

☆ 2

1

2

3

A Name these solid shapes:

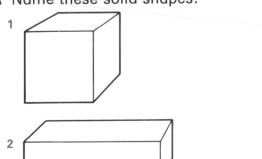

1

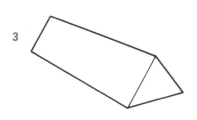

2

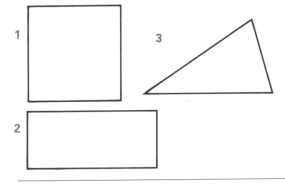

3

B Name these shapes:

1

2

3

C Part of each rectangle is hidden. Write the length of each side:

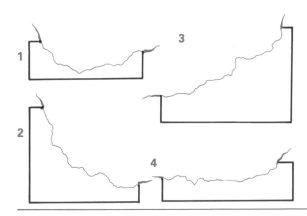

1

2

3

4

D Are these angles right angles? Write **yes** or **no**:

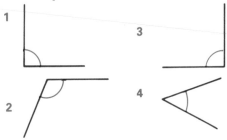

1

2

3

4

E Where will the arrow be after the turn?

1 turn 1
right angle
clockwise

2 turn 2
right angles
anti-clockwise

3 turn 3
right angles
anti-clockwise

4 turn 2
right angles
anti-clockwise

F How many:

1 squares?
2 rectangles?
3 triangles?
4 circles?

UNITS

	0	1	2	3	4	5	6	7	8	9
0	0	1	2	3	4	5	6	7	8	9
1	10	11	12	13	14	15	16	17	18	19
2	20	21	22	23	24	25	26	27	28	29
T 3	30	31	32	33	34	35	36	37	38	39
E 4	40	41	42	43	44	45	46	47	48	49
N 5	50	51	52	53	54	55	56	57	58	59
S 6	60	61	62	63	64	65	66	67	68	69
7	70	71	72	73	74	75	76	77	78	79
8	80	81	82	83	84	85	86	87	88	89
9	90	91	92	93	94	95	96	97	98	99

How many sweets altogether?

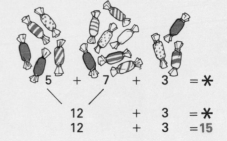

5 + 7 + 3 = *

12 + 3 = *

12 + 3 = 15

You can add the groups in a different order:

7+5+3= *   3+5+7= *

12 + 3=   8 + 7= *

12 + 3=15   8 + 7=15

The easiest order   7+3+5= *
is to make 10 first: 10 +5= *
                         10 +5=15

A Use the number square if you need to. Write numbers for *'s:

☆ 6+7= * 13

1 7+6= *   6 5+11= *
2 5+9= *   7 11+5= *
3 9+5= *   8 14+6= *
4 8+7= *   9 6+14= *
5 7+8= *

B Write numbers for *'s:

☆ 6+5= * 11   5 4+8= *
1 16+5= *   6 14+8= *
2 26+5= *   7 24+8= *
3 36+5= *   8 34+8= *
4 46+5= *   9 44+8= *

C Write numbers for *'s:

☆ 5+10= * 15   5 7+20= *
1 15+10= *   6 17+20= *
2 25+10= *   7 27+20= *
3 35+10= *   8 37+20= *
4 45+10= *   9 47+20= *

D Write numbers for *'s:

☆ 6+5+4= * 15

1 8+3+2= *   7 7+2+8= *
2 7+5+5= *   8 5+4+5= *
3 4+7+3= *   9 2+9+8= *
4 9+2+1= *   10 6+4+6= *
5 8+6+4= *   11 7+4+6= *
6 6+3+4= *   12 7+10+2= *

E Answer these:

☆ With 3 darts Jim scores 8, 3 and 7. How many does he score altogether? 18

1 Jill spends 3p, 6p and 7p. How much does she spend altogether?

2 Jo has 4 marbles. He wins 5 and buys 6 more. How many marbles does he have altogether?

3 A dog makes 8 barks, 3 barks and 7 barks. How many barks altogether?

4 Fred saves 8p, 2p and 3p. How much does he save altogether?

5 With 3 darts Ann scores 6, 5 and 5. How many does she score altogether?

Add together 23 and 6:

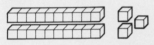

Tens	Units
2	3
+	6
2	9

2 tens   9 units

Martin has 24 stamps.
He is given 4 more stamps.
How many stamps does he have altogether?

T	U
2	4
+	4
2	8

He has **28** stamps altogether.

A How many altogether?

Tens	Units
3	4
+	5
3	9

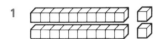

1

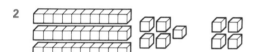

2

3

4

C Use addition to answer these:

☆ Ann has 12 books. She buys 7 more. How many books does she have altogether?

T	U
1	2
+	7
1	9

1 John has 2 mice. He buys 4 more. How many mice does he have altogether?

2 Joy has 16 stamps. She collects 3 more. How many stamps does she have altogether?

3 Jack has 24 fish. He catches 5 more. How many fish does he have altogether?

4 Jill has 52p. She is given 7p more. How much does she have altogether?

B Copy and complete:

☆
Tens	Units
5	2
+	6

Tens	Units
5	2
+	6
5	8

1
Tens	Units
2	6
+	3

2
Tens	Units
5	2
+	7

3
Tens	Units
3	4
+	5

4
Tens	Units
2	5
+	3

5
Tens	Units
4	2
+	6

6
Tens	Units
7	4
+	4

D Copy and complete:

☆
T	U
3	2
+	6

T	U
3	2
+	6
3	8

1
T	U
2	4
+	3

2
T	U
3	4
+	4

3
T	U
6	1
+	7

4
T	U
2	0
+	9

5
T	U
4	0
+	8

6
T	U
9	3
+	4

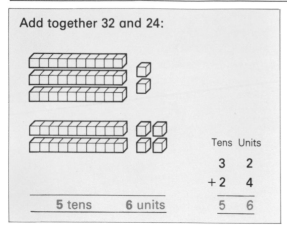

Add together 32 and 24:

Tens	Units
3	2
+2	4

5 tens   **6** units | 5 | 6 |

Mary has 14 fish.
She buys 13 more.
How many fish does
she have altogether?

T	U
1	4
+1	3
2	7

**She has
27 fish
altogether.**

A How many altogether?

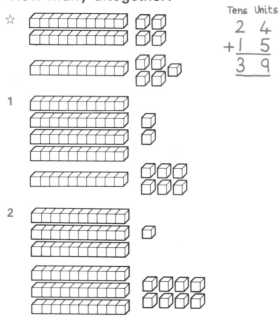

☆
Tens	Units
2	4
+1	5
3	9

1

2

C Use addition to answer these:

☆ Mike has 25 marbles.
He wins 14 more.
How many marbles
does he have altogether?

T	U
2	5
+1	4
3	9

1 A garage has 36 cars. 13 more are
brought in. How many cars in the
garage altogether?

2 A dog eats 24 biscuits, and then 25
more. How many biscuits does the
dog eat altogether?

3 Joy makes 34 skips and then another
44 skips. How many skips does she
make altogether?

4 Jack runs 60 metres and then
another 36 metres. How many
metres does he run altogether?

B Copy and complete:

☆
Tens	Units
3	2
+2	6

Tens	Units
3	2
+2	6
5	8

1
Tens	Units
5	3
+1	4

3
Tens	Units
3	5
+3	2

5
Tens	Units
5	5
+3	2

2
Tens	Units
6	0
+2	9

4
Tens	Units
8	6
+1	2

6
Tens	Units
4	2
+3	6

D Copy and complete:

☆
T	U
3	5
+4	2

T	U
3	5
+4	2
7	7

1
T	U
2	3
+3	5

3
T	U
1	8
+6	1

5
T	U
4	2
+3	7

2
T	U
4	4
+3	3

4
T	U
2	7
+5	2

6
T	U
6	6
+3	3

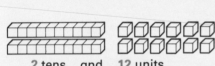

2 tens and **12 units**.

If you change 10 units to 1 ten you have:

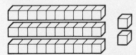

3 tens and 2 units.

So: **2 tens** and **12 units**
  =**3 tens** and **2 units**.

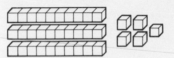

3 tens and 5 units.

If you change 1 ten to 10 units you have:

2 tens and 15 units.
So: **3 tens** and **5 units**
   =**2 tens** and **15 units**.

A Use apparatus if you need to.
Change 10 units to 1 ten.
Write numbers for ✱'s:

☆ 3 tens 14 units=4 tens and 4 units

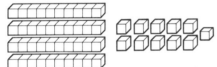

1 4 tens 11 units= ✱ tens and ✱ units

2 2 tens 16 units= ✱ tens and ✱ units

3 3 tens 13 units= ✱ tens and ✱ units

B Change 10 units to 1 ten.
Write numbers for ✱'s:

☆ 4 tens and 16 units=5 tens and 6 units

1 1 ten and 15 units= ✱ tens ✱ units

2 3 tens and 18 units= ✱ tens ✱ units

3 6 tens and 14 units= ✱ tens ✱ units

4 5 tens and 17 units= ✱ tens ✱ units

5 2 tens and 19 units= ✱ tens ✱ units

C Use apparatus if you need to.
Change 1 ten to 10 units.
Write numbers for ✱'s:

☆ 2 tens 3 units=1 ten and 13 units

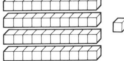

1 4 tens 1 unit= ✱ tens ✱ units

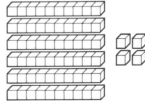

2 6 tens 4 units= ✱ tens ✱ units

3 3 tens 7 units= ✱ tens ✱ units

D Change 1 ten to 10 units.
Write numbers for ✱'s:

☆ 3 tens 8 units=2 tens and 18 units

1 2 tens 4 units= ✱ ten ✱ units

2 4 tens 2 units= ✱ tens ✱ units

3 7 tens 5 units= ✱ tens ✱ units

4 6 tens 2 units= ✱ tens ✱ units

5 5 tens 6 units= ✱ tens ✱ units

Add together 34 and 8:

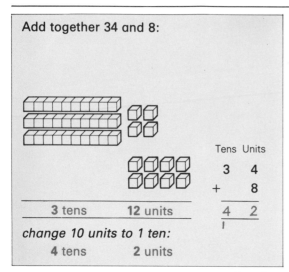

	Tens	Units
	3	4
+		8
	4	2
	₁	

3 tens 12 units

change 10 units to 1 ten:

4 tens 2 units

Trevor has 19 mice.
He buys 6 more.
How many mice does he have altogether?

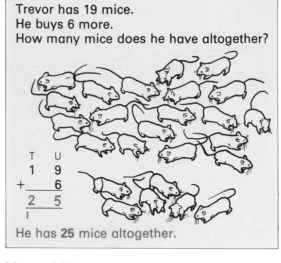

	T	U
	1	9
+		6
	2	5

He has **25** mice altogether.

A How many altogether?

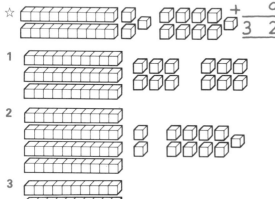

☆
	Tens	Units
	2	3
+		9
	3	2

1

2

3

C Use addition to answer these:

☆ Jeff eats 27 nuts.
He then eats 5 more.
How many nuts does
he eat altogether?

	T	U
	2	7
+		5
	3	2

1 Tom has 7 sweets. He buys 6 more.
How many sweets does he have
altogether?

2 Beverley has 37 pence. She is given
5 pence more. How many
pence does she have altogether?

3 David has 38 pencils. He is given
7 more. How many pencils
does he have altogether?

B Copy and complete:

☆
Tens	Units
2	7
+	9

Tens	Units
2	7
+	9
3	6

1
Tens	Units
5	4
+	7

2
Tens	Units
6	5
+	6

3
Tens	Units
4	7
+	8

4
Tens	Units
6	9
+	7

5
Tens	Units
5	8
+	6

6
Tens	Units
7	5
+	9

D Copy and complete:

☆
T	U
3	5
+	7

T	U
3	5
+	7
4	2

1
T	U
4	7
+	8

2
T	U
6	3
+	9

3
T	U
5	6
+	5

4
T	U
4	7
+4	6

5
T	U
8	2
+	8

6
T	U
3	8
+	5

Addition

Add together 47 and 16:

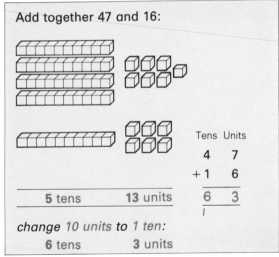

Tens	Units
4	7
+1	6
6	3

5 tens   13 units

change 10 units *to* 1 ten:

6 tens   3 units

Jeff eats 26 nuts. He then eats 15 more. How many nuts does he eat altogether?

T	U
2	6
+1	5
4	1

He eats **41** nuts altogether.

A How many altogether?

☆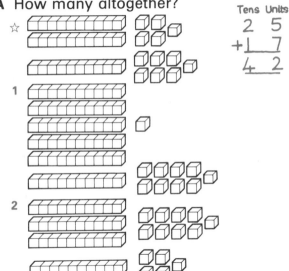

Tens	Units
2	5
+1	7
4	2

1

2

C Use addition to answer these:

☆ David has 35 pencils. He is given 17 more. How many pencils does he have altogether?

T	U
3	5
+1	7
5	2

1 Sue has 37 sweets. She buys 18 more. How many sweets does she have altogether?

2 A donkey eats 29 carrots and then 14 more. How many carrots altogether?

3 Jack scores 43 and 49 at darts. How many did he score altogether?

4 In Class 3 there are 12 girls and 19 boys. How many children altogether?

5 A piece of wood is 38 cm long. A second piece is 27 cm long. How long are the two pieces together?

B Copy and complete:

☆
Tens	Units
6	4
+2	8

Tens	Units
6	4
+2	8
9	2

1
Tens	Units
3	5
+2	8

2
Tens	Units
4	7
+3	9

3
Tens	Units
1	7
+5	8

4
Tens	Units
6	9
+1	8

5
Tens	Units
5	4
+3	6

6
Tens	Units
2	7
+2	7

D Copy and complete:

☆
T	U
2	3
+3	8

T	U
2	3
+3	8
6	1

1
T	U
4	4
+4	7

2
T	U
7	8
+1	9

3
T	U
6	3
+2	7

4
T	U
5	5
+2	7

5
T	U
4	7
+3	7

6
T	U
2	9
+6	6

If the police car follows the smallest
answer at each junction, who is caught?

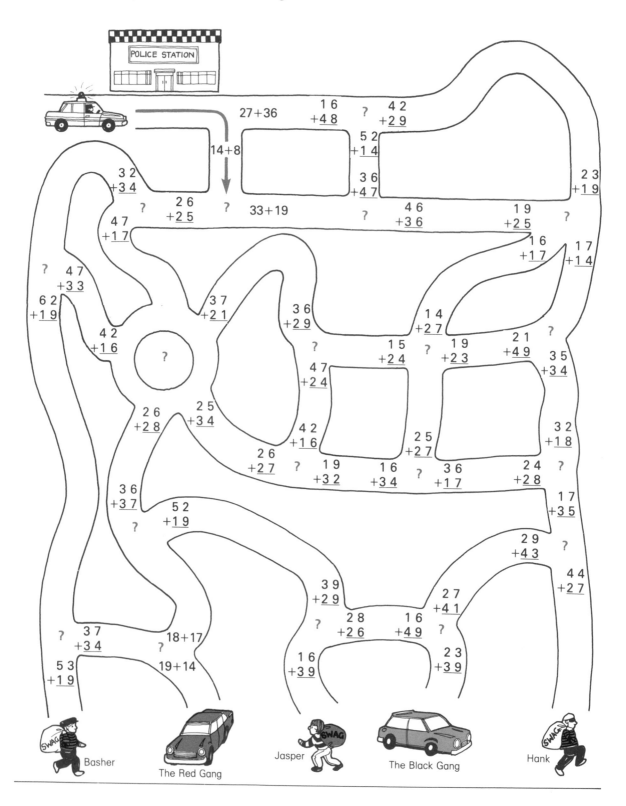

Basher

The Red Gang

Jasper

The Black Gang

Hank

Subtraction

0	1	2	3	4	5	6	7	8	9
10	11	12	13	14	15	16	17	18	19
20	21	22	23	24	25	26	27	28	29
30	31	32	33	34	35	36	37	38	39
40	41	42	43	44	45	46	47	48	49
50	51	52	53	54	55	56	57	58	59
60	61	62	63	64	65	66	67	68	69
70	71	72	73	74	75	76	77	78	79
80	81	82	83	84	85	86	87	88	89
90	91	92	93	94	95	96	97	98	99

A Use the number square if you need to.
Write numbers for ✱'s:

☆ $10-8=$ ✱ 2   6 $12-4=$ ✱
1 $10-7=$ ✱   7 $12-5=$ ✱
2 $10-6=$ ✱   8 $12-6=$ ✱
3 $10-5=$ ✱   9 $12-7=$ ✱
4 $10-4=$ ✱   10 $12-8=$ ✱
5 $10-3=$ ✱   11 $12-9=$ ✱

B Write numbers for ✱'s:

☆ $6-4=$ ✱ 2   6 $9-2=$ ✱
1 $16-4=$ ✱   7 $19-2=$ ✱
2 $26-4=$ ✱   8 $29-2=$ ✱
3 $36-4=$ ✱   9 $39-2=$ ✱
4 $46-4=$ ✱   10 $49-2=$ ✱
5 $56-4=$ ✱   11 $59-2=$ ✱

C Write numbers for ✱'s:

☆ $17-10=$ ✱ 7   6 $92-10=$ ✱
1 $27-10=$ ✱   7 $92-20=$ ✱
2 $37-10=$ ✱   8 $92-30=$ ✱
3 $47-10=$ ✱   9 $92-40=$ ✱
4 $57-10=$ ✱   10 $92-50=$ ✱
5 $67-10=$ ✱   11 $92-60=$ ✱

D Use subtraction to find the **difference**
between:

☆ 9 and 3 6   6 4 and 14
1 10 and 3   7 4 and 15
2 11 and 3   8 4 and 16
3 12 and 3   9 4 and 17
4 13 and 3   10 4 and 18
5 14 and 3   11 4 and 19

E Use **subtraction** to answer these:

☆ There are 19 flowers in a garden.
8 are picked. How many are left? 11

1 A piece of spaghetti
is 18 cm long.
Lucy eats 7 cm.
What length is left?

2 There are 16 cars in a garage. 5 are
sold. How many are left?

3 Mandy has 19 sweets. She eats 9.
How many has she left?

4 A spider catches 16 flies. It eats 7.
How many are left?

F Use **subtraction** to answer these:

☆ Mary is 9. Her brother is 18. How
many years difference in their ages?
9

1 The score in a
football match was
Reds 6 Greens 8.
What was the
difference in scores?

SCORE BOARD

REDS 6

GREENS 8

2 A circus has 18 dogs and 4 horses.
How many more dogs than horses?

3 Jack is 8 and Ben is 14. How many
years difference in their ages?

4 A shop has 20 blue cases and 7 red
cases. How many more blue cases
than red cases?

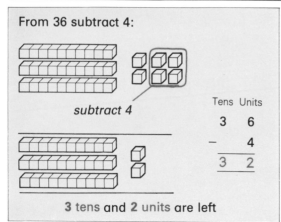

From 36 subtract 4:

subtract 4

Tens	Units
3	6
−	4
3	2

3 tens and 2 units are left

A How many are left when you subtract 5 from each group:

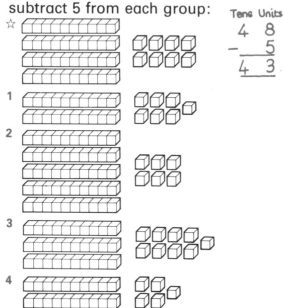

☆
Tens	Units
4	8
−	5
4	3

1

2

3

4

B Copy and complete:

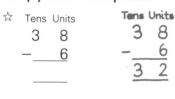

☆
Tens	Units
3	8
−	6

Tens Units
3	8
−	6
3	2

1
Tens	Units
4	5
−	4

3
Tens	Units
2	4
−	3

5
Tens	Units
6	8
−	7

2
Tens	Units
3	9
−	7

4
Tens	Units
9	5
−	5

6
Tens	Units
5	7
−	5

C Use **subtraction** to answer these. Find how many left if:

☆ Bill has 15 frogs and 3 get away.

T	U
1	5
−	3
1	2

1 Trevor has 47 marbles and loses 6.

2 Dan has 56 stamps and gives away 5.

3 Sam has 25 chips and eats 4.

4 Denise has 19 balloons and 7 burst.

5 Anna has 28 sweets and eats 7.

6 Paul has 37 crisps and eats 6.

7 Ann has 69 books and gives away 6.

8 Jo has 77 comics and gives away 7.

D Use subtraction to answer these. What is the **difference** in ages if:

T	U
2	9
−	7
2	2

☆ Sally is 7 and her mother is 29?

1 Lucy is 6 and her father is 38?

2 Ann is 5 and her father is 29?

3 Jack is 19 and Jim is 8?

4 Sally is 17 and Alice is 7?

5 Jenny is 8 and her mother is 29?

6 Mr Brown is 36 and his son is 4?

7 Sharon is 2 and her father is 26?

8 John is 7 and his mother is 28?

E Copy and complete:

☆
T	U
5	7
−	4

T	U
5	7
−	4
5	3

1
T	U
3	5
−	3

3
T	U
7	5.
−	4

5
T	U
2	9
−	6

2
T	U
5	9
−	7

4
T	U
5	8
−	5

6
T	U
7	8
−	4

Subtraction

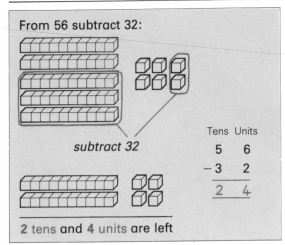

From 56 subtract 32:

subtract 32

	Tens	Units
	5	6
−	3	2
	2	4

2 tens and 4 units are left

A How many are left when you subtract 13 from each group:

☆
	Tens	Units
	3	7
−	1	3
	2	4

1

2

3

B Copy and complete:

☆
Tens	Units
4	5
−2	3

Tens	Units
4	5
−2	3
2	2

1
Tens	Units
6	9
−2	6

3
Tens	Units
7	9
−2	4

5
Tens	Units
6	9
−4	7

2
Tens	Units
5	4
−3	1

4
Tens	Units
9	4
−7	2

6
Tens	Units
8	9
−5	0

C Use subtraction to answer these:

☆ Find how many left if: there are 37 birds on a branch and 14 fly away.

	T	U
	3	7
−	1	4
	2	3

1 A dog has 49 biscuits and eats 27.

2 Bill has 59 coins and gives away 18.

3 Alan has 36 marbles and loses 24.

4 A rose has 24 petals and 10 fall off.

5 A bird catches 27 worms and eats 14.

D These are the scores in a darts game:

SCORE BOARD	
JOHN	58
MARY	24
PAUL	35
SHARON	89
BILL	47

Use subtraction to find the difference in scores between:

	T	U
	5	8
−	2	4
	3	4

☆ Mary and John

1 John and Paul   5 Mary and Paul

2 Paul and Sharon   6 Bill and Sharon

3 Sharon and Mary   7 John and Sharon

4 Mary and Bill   8 Bill and John

E Copy and complete:

☆
	T	U
	4	9
−	3	2

	T	U
	4	9
−	3	2
	1	7

1
T	U
3	7
−1	4

3
T	U
9	6
−3	5

5
T	U
5	7
−2	7

2
T	U
5	9
−2	2

4
T	U
8	4
−3	3

6
T	U
9	6
−1	1

From 32 subtract 8:

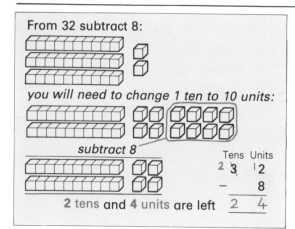

you will need to change 1 ten to 10 units:

subtract 8

Tens	Units
2 3	¹2
−	8
2	4

2 tens and **4 units** are left

A How many left in each group when you subtract 7:

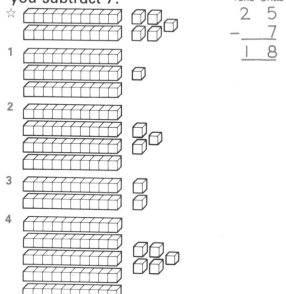

Tens	Units
2	5
−	7
1	8

C Use subtraction to answer these.
Find how many left if:

☆ John has 42 stamps and gives away 9.

T	U
4	2
−	9
3	3

1 Ann has 27 books and gives away 8.
2 Sarah has 32 toys and gives away 9.
3 Bob has 21 mice and sells 6.
4 Tom has 30 stamps and loses 4.
5 Jill has 24 dolls and gives away 7.

D Use subtraction to find the difference between the number of:

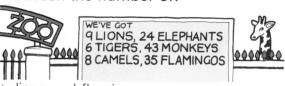

WE'VE GOT
9 LIONS, 24 ELEPHANTS
6 TIGERS, 43 MONKEYS
8 CAMELS, 35 FLAMINGOS

☆ lions and flamingos
1 monkeys and tigers
2 tigers and elephants
3 camels and flamingos
4 elephants and lions
5 camels and monkeys
6 elephants and camels

T	U
3	5
−	9
2	6

B Copy and complete:

☆
Tens	Units
5	6
−	9

Tens	Units
5	6
−	9
4	7

1
Tens	Units
4	1
−	6

3
Tens	Units
3	5
−	8

5
Tens	Units
6	2
−	4

2
Tens	Units
3	6
−	8

4
Tens	Units
2	2
−	9

6
Tens	Units
4	0
−	4

E Copy and complete:

☆
T	U
3	4
−	9

T	U
3	4
−	9
2	5

1
T	U
6	1
−	7

3
T	U
3	2
−	6

5
T	U
3	7
−	9

2
T	U
5	4
−	8

4
T	U
4	3
−	5

6
T	U
6	0
−	7

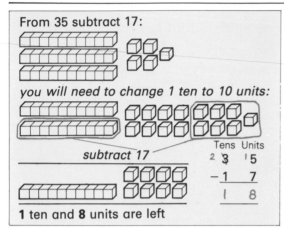

From 35 subtract 17:

you will need to change 1 ten to 10 units:

subtract 17

	Tens	Units
	²3̶	¹5
−	1	7
	1	8

1 ten and **8 units** are left

A How many left in each group when you subtract 19:

☆

	Tens	Units
	4	6
−	1	9
	2	7

1

2

3

4

B Copy and complete:

☆

Tens	Units
3	3
−1	5

T	U
3	3
−1	5
1	8

1
Tens	Units
4	2
−1	7

2
Tens	Units
3	5
−1	6

3
Tens	Units
2	1
−1	8

4
Tens	Units
5	4
−2	8

5
Tens	Units
6	2
−3	7

6
Tens	Units
8	4
−6	7

C Use subtraction to answer these.
Find how many pence left if:

	T	U
	3	2
−	1	4
	1	8

☆ John has 32p and spends 14p.   18p left

1 Sally has 51p and spends 16p.

2 Jill has 37p and spends 28p.

3 Bob has 64p and spends 38p.

4 Sharon has 76p and spends 57p

5 Jack has 82p and spends 43p.

D

vase	bicycle	chair	picture	lamp
£28	£71	£47	£39	£19

Use subtraction to answer these.
How many pounds difference in cost between:

	T	U
	4	7
−	2	8
	1	9

☆ a vase and a chair?

1 a lamp and a chair?   £19 difference

2 a picture and a chair?

3 a picture and a bicycle?

4 a chair and a bicycle?

5 a vase and a bicycle?

6 a lamp and a vase?

E Copy and complete:

☆
T	U
4	2
−1	6

T	U
4	2
−1	6
2	6

1
T	U
3	1
−1	7

2
T	U
4	2
−2	3

3
T	U
6	3
−3	8

4
T	U
8	6
−2	9

5
T	U
9	6
−5	8

6
T	U
7	0
−3	4

A Use **addition** to find:

☆ the number of loaves altogether.

```
  T U
  4 8
+ 2 4
─────
  7 2
```

48 loaves   24 loaves

1 The number of toys altogether.

39 toys   46 toys

2 The number of fish altogether.

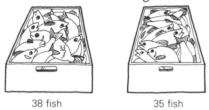

38 fish   35 fish

3 The number of pies altogether.

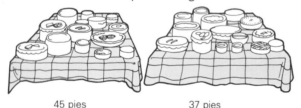

45 pies   37 pies

4 The number of leaves altogether.

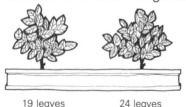

19 leaves   24 leaves

5 The number of flowers altogether.

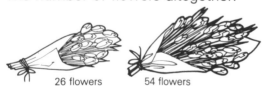

26 flowers   54 flowers

B Use **subtraction** to find:

☆ how many years difference in age between Fred and Jane?

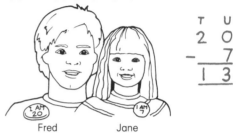

Fred   Jane

```
  T U
  2 0
−   7
─────
  1 3
```

1 How many metres difference in length between rope A and rope B?

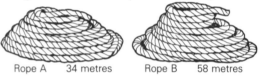

Rope A   34 metres   Rope B   58 metres

2 The difference in pounds between Mike's money and Sally's money?

£24   £32

3 How many apples are left when 24 are taken from this box:

60 apples

4 The length of string left when 35 centimetres are cut off?

length of
string: 82 centimetres

5 How much is left if you have 92p but spend 48p?

Revision for pages 82–94

A Copy and complete:

```
1  T U      4  T U      7  T U
   2 3         4 7         2 3
 +4 5       +4 2        +4 2

2  T U      5  T U      8  T U
   3 2         1 3         5 5
 +5 7       +3 6        +4 4

3  T U      6  T U      9  T U
   2 3         4 4         6 3
 +7 6       +3 2        +2 5
```

B Use addition to answer these:

1 Mike has 15 marbles. He wins 14 more. How many marbles does he have altogether?

2 Mary has 23 pence. She is given 28 pence more. How much does she have altogether?

3 Bill walks 39 metres and then another 46 metres. How many metres does he walk altogether?

4 There are 26 fish in a tank. 7 more are put in. How many fish in the tank altogether?

5 Jill has 29 toys. She is given 12 more. How many toys does she have altogether?

C Copy and complete:

```
1  T U      3  T U      5  T U
   4 3         6 1         5 3
 -   8       -   9       -   6

2  T U      4  T U      6  T U
   3 4         7 2         4 1
 -   7       -   5       -   3
```

D Copy and complete:

```
1  T U      3  T U      5  T U
   9 4         4 7         9 3
 -2 3        -2 5        -2 3

2  T U      4  T U      6  T U
   6 8         6 4         8 7
 -2 7        -3 3        -6 4
```

E Use subtraction to answer these. How many left if:

1 John has 16 balloons and 7 burst.

2 Anna has 36 crisps and eats 9.

3 Jill has 44 coins and gives away 15.

4 There are 58 straws in a box and 12 are used.

5 Ben has 41 mice and sells 26.

6 35 people are on a bus and 17 get off.

7 Mrs James bakes 43 cakes and 27 are eaten.

8 Kate has 32 sweets and gives away 18.

9 A book shop has 53 comics and 19 are sold.

10 A clown has 76 balloons and gives away 48.

11 There are 52 children in the Hall and 17 leave.

F Copy and complete:

```
1  T U      3  T U      5  T U
   6 1         7 3         3 0
 -2 9        -3 7        -1 7

2  T U      4  T U      6  T U
   5 4         6 2         6 0
 -3 6        -2 6        -1 9
```

Find the number that falls into each bucket:

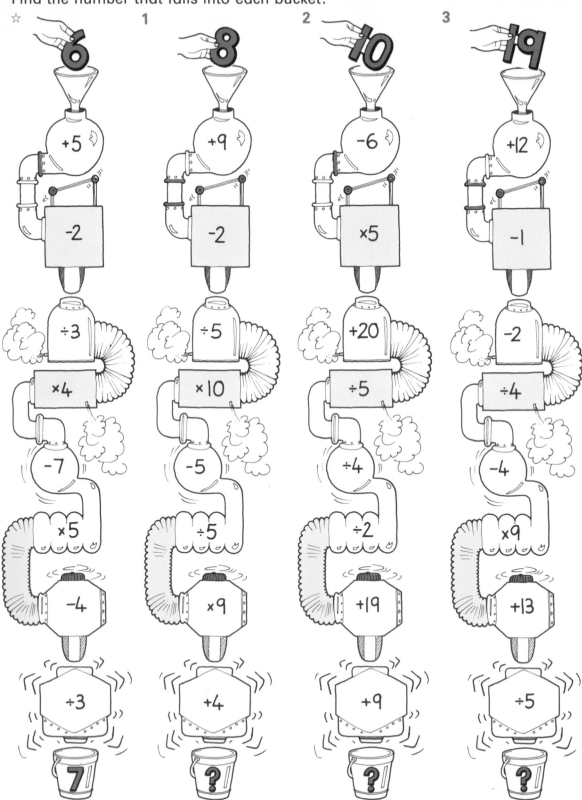

☆ 6, +5, -2, ÷3, ×4, -7, ×5, -4, ÷3, bucket: **7**

1 8, +9, -2, ÷5, ×10, -5, ÷5, ×9, +4, bucket: **?**

2 10, -6, ×5, +20, ÷5, ÷4, ÷2, +19, +9, bucket: **?**

3 19, +12, -1, -2, ÷4, -4, ×9, +13, ÷5, bucket: **?**